One-Dimensional Queer

One-Dimensional Queer

Roderick A. Ferguson

polity

First published in 2019 by Polity Press

Polity Press
65 Bridge Street
Cambridge CB2 1UR, UK

Polity Press
101 Station Landing
Suite 300
Medford, MA 02155, USA

ISBN-13: 978-1-5095-2355-9
ISBN-13: 978-1-5095-2356-6 (pb)

A catalogue record for this book is available from the British Library.

Library of Congress Cataloging-in-Publication Data

Names: Ferguson, Roderick A., author.
Title: One-dimensional queer / Roderick Ferguson.
Description: Medford, MA : Polity, 2018. | Includes bibliographical references
    and index.
Identifiers: LCCN 2018019548 (print) | LCCN 2018034841 (ebook) |
    ISBN 9781509523597 (Epub) | ISBN 9781509523559 (hardback) |
    ISBN 9781509523566 (paperback)
Subjects: LCSH: Gay rights. | Gay liberation movement. | Social change. |
    BISAC: SOCIAL SCIENCE / Gender Studies.
Classification: LCC HQ76.5 (ebook) | LCC HQ76.5 .F47 2018 (print) |
    DDC 323.3/264–dc23
LC record available at https://lccn.loc.gov/2018019548

Typeset in 11 on 15 pt Adobe Garamond
by Toppan Best-set Premedia Limited
Printed and bound in the United Kingdom by Clays Ltd, Elcograph S.p.A.

For further information on Polity, visit our website: politybooks.com

CONTENTS

Introduction

Roland Emmerich's 2015 film *Stonewall* purports to tell the story of that eventful day of the gay uprising at the Stonewall Inn in 1969, doing so with a not so agreeable twist. Rather than basing the story on the racially and ethnically diverse group of queens who started the uprising, the film makes a young cisgender white man named Danny the origin and center of that fateful day. According to *The Guardian*'s entertainment writer Nigel Smith, Emmerich "defended both his narrative decisions and choice of lead, saying that he'd made the movie for as wide an audience as possible, and that 'straight-acting' Danny was an 'easy in' for heterosexual viewers" (Smith, 2015). There were apparently other "easy in's" for the film as well. It was "easy" to cast the queens as pre-political sirens who erupted only after Danny prompted them. It was also "easy" to imagine that the riots began with only heterosexist oppression in mind, this despite the fact that Danny leads the crowd in a chant of "Gay Power," a category that could only exist because of the nearness of the black revolution.

In his review, Smith noted that even the trailer for the film "worried many with what appeared to be a 'white-washed' take on a diverse group of people," with some calling for a boycott of the film. Despite the appropriate disapproval that critics heaped onto the film, Emmerich's *Stonewall* was actually following a convention long in the making. In fact, we might say that the film and its narrative of Stonewall are part of the casualties not only of the mainstreaming of Stonewall but of gay liberation itself.

For the longest time we have believed that queer liberation arose as a single-issue event that was simply about sexuality. Hence, we have told ourselves that queer politics came to issues of race, colonization, incarceration, and capitalism later in its development. This book tells a different story, one in which a multidimensional host of concerns were there from the very beginning only to be excised later on. In fact, since the late sixties – from the Stonewall uprisings even – the intersectional interests of gay liberation expressed a politics that would try to relate issues of sexuality, race, class, and gender to one another. Hence, part of the book locates gay liberation within a political and intellectual context that was trying to find ways for various struggles to join forces, noting that gay liberation actually emerged out of those efforts of affiliation. *One-Dimensional Queer* goes on to show that multidimensional and intersectional interests were overtaken by single-issue formulations of queer politics, formulations that would promote liberal capitalist ideologies. Hence, as a multidimensional gay politics transitioned to a single-issue and one-dimensional platform, the meaning of freedom for queer and transgender folks and minorities, in general, shifted radically.

As a critique of the dominant way of narrating queer political histories, the book problematizes the presumption that gay liberation was always and already a single-issue politics. It does so by taking inspiration from the work of groups such as the Gay Liberation Front, Street Transvestite Action Revolutionaries, the Combahee River Collective, Third World Gay Revolution, Gay Latino Alliance, DYKETACTICS! and so on. Challenging the presumption that intersectional activism among queers is a recent phenomenon, the book instead argues that such political models were not recent at all but constitutive of the political aspirations of "early" gay liberation.

As intersectional activists, gay liberationists were putting to use the political discourses that were being crafted by various progressive struggles, discourses that took the relational nature of progressive struggles as the basis of political interventions. Part of the relational politics involved an interest in disrupting the liberal notion that forms of difference are inherently antagonistic to each other, that difference itself was a source of separation and antagonism. The book, therefore, is an observance of what Audre Lorde called the "institutionalized rejection of difference" (Lorde, 2007, p. 115).

The one-dimensionality of queerness

The book's title and inquiry are taken from Herbert Marcuse's classic 1964 text *One-Dimensional Man*. Like this one, Marcuse's book tried to comprehend the ideological foundations that allowed industrial society to proceed without opposition. For Marcuse, the repressions of industrial society were qualitatively different from the repressions in other forms of society. As he put it, "This repression, so different from what characterized the preceding, less developed stages of our society, operates today not from a position of natural and technical immaturity but rather from a position of strength" (Marcuse, 1991, p. xlii). Describing how industrial society achieves ideological dominance, he argued, "Technical progress, extended to a whole system of domination and coordination, creates forms of life (and of power) which appear to reconcile the forces opposing the system and to defeat or refute all protest in the name of the historical prospects of freedom from toil and domination"

4

(Marcuse, 1991, p. xliv). Here, Marcuse pointed to how the technical resources of industrial society are maneuvered to disqualify opposition, the result of which is a society in which "former antagonists" are united in an "overriding interest in the preservation and improvement of the institutional status quo" (Marcuse, 1991, p. xlv).

One-Dimensional Queer is similarly concerned with how incorporating queerness into US state discourse and American capitalism was aided by a single-issue articulation of queer politics. In doing so, the book casts a critical eye on the presumed signs of gay progress – the extension of rights to queers and the inclusion of queers within capitalist economic visions. For Marcuse, one-dimensionality represented the containment of social change inasmuch as technical progress was seen as providing people in society with everything that they needed. In the context of the normalization of queerness, one-dimensionality designates the containment of social change inasmuch as the mainstreaming of gay identity and sexuality (i.e. grooming them for the needs of state and capital) are understood to be signs of social progress.

For Marcuse, one-dimensionality denoted people's surrender to the given social and institutional landscape, a surrender that was part of the very intention of advanced industrial society. Describing this ethos, he argued, "Contemporary society seems to be capable of containing social change – qualitative change which would establish essentially different institutions, a new direction of the productive process, new modes of human existence. This containment of social change is perhaps the most singular achievement of advanced industrial society" (Marcuse, 1991, p. xliv). From Marcuse, we get a sense of one-dimensionality as the conflation of state and capital's needs with personal needs, the understanding of capitalist logics as the epitome of reason, the systematic and deliberate negation of social alternatives, and the acquiescence to the given social and institutional order. This book attempts to show how the mainstreaming of gay liberation attempted to turn queerness into an endorsement of state and capital as the satisfiers of queer needs, as the incarnations of reason, and as the reasons to make peace with the world that capitalism helped to bring about.

The threat of the multidimensional

If one-dimensionality, according to Marcuse, identified those social processes that attempt to restrict social transformations, countering one-dimensionality meant producing people and collectivities that "[refuse] to accept the given universe of facts as the final context of validation" (Marcuse, 1991, p. xliii). Critical theory was part of that enterprise of refusal. As Marcuse argued, "To investigate the roots of these developments and examine their historical alternatives is part of the aim of a critical theory of contemporary society, a theory which analyzes society in the light of its used and unused or abused capabilities for improving the human condition" (Marcuse, 1991, p. xlii).

This book attempts to show how intersectional and multidimensional queer struggles (i.e. ones that addressed the overlaps between differences of race, class, gender, and transgender) were key ingredients of that refusal. As the book will show, groups such as Street Transvestite Action Revolutionaries, Third World Gay Revolution, the Combahee River Collective, and DYKETACTICS! offered analyses of interlocking and intersecting oppressions as provocations for "improving the human condition" and imagining new kinds of peoples and collectivities. Such groups represent the historical evidence of queer and trans capacities to think and live beyond the gender, sexual, racial, and class prescriptions of the world that we have inherited.

In an effort to show how those capacities were regulated and suppressed, the book attempts to show how the intersectional and multidimensional aspects of gay liberation suffered a backlash by single-issue political and economic forces. For instance, the book analyzes how insulating the push for gay liberation from other progressive struggles was no academic matter. Indeed, driving a wedge between queer politics and other progressive formations worked to tie queer politics to an investment in state practices and capitalist expansion.

The book also contends that divorcing queer liberation from political struggles around race, poverty, capitalism, and colonization helped to conceal the historical and political complexity of queer liberation itself. Put simply, by mainstreaming queerness – making it conform to civic ideals of respectability, national-belonging, and support for the free market – gay rights and gay capital helped to renew racial, ethnic, class, gender, and sexual exclusions. Hence, the book's main inquiry concerns how gay rights and gay capital promoted forms of racial, gender, and class exclusions that left people of color, the poor, and queers of color to be the victims of those exclusions. Examining queer liberation's cleavage from political struggles around racial, gender, transgender, and class equalities means that the book necessarily traces how queerness entered the mainstream after its radicalization in the sixties and seventies, producing a historical moment in which social exclusions within the US were increasingly assisted by the mainstreaming of homosexuality. To this end, the book argues that the struggle between an intersectional

and multi-issue gay liberation versus a single-issue politics was a political event of the first order, one that has
shaped queer politics and queer life to this day.

The political and economic effects of single-issue sexuality

Attending to the ways that gay rights and gay capital
subjugated this intersectional history, the book argues that
the rise of a single-issue (i.e. one-dimensional) model of
queer politics has inspired several political developments
concerning the meaning and itineraries of queer politics.
To begin with, that rise authorized a historical narrative
that naturalized a single-issue political model as the origin
of queer politics. The ascendancy of a single-issue notion
of gay liberation also put in place a gay rights agenda
that constructed the critique of racism, capitalism, the
state, and their overlaps as outside the normal and practical interests of gay liberation. It relegated transgender
histories and politics to the dustbin of queer history,
and it provided momentum to the argument that social
and political freedom for queers would come through
capitalist economic formations. Rather than approach
this single-issue narrative as a discrete discourse that
only pertains to queer and trans folks, the book shows

how the single-issue framework has had broad political and economic reach.

One obvious example of the one-dimensional orientation that queer politics has assumed is the marriage equality movement. For instance, the historian and theorist Lisa Duggan observed in 2012 before the Court's ruling on *Obergefell v. Hodges*, "Marriage equality has become the singularly representative issue for the mainstream LGBT [lesbian, gay, bisexual, transgender] rights movement, often standing in for all the political aspirations of queer people" (Duggan, 2012). Duggan points to how marriage narrows the political universe of queer communities, a narrowing that is tied to a social and intimate narrowing as well. Referring to how the expansion of intimate cultures was part of gay liberation agendas in the past, Duggan argues, "But rather than continue to expand the forms of partnership and household recognition begun by the LGBT movement in the 1970s, the marriage equality campaign has resulted in a contraction of options" (Duggan, 2012). Duggan goes on to note how marriage equality cannibalized all other political alternatives: "Whether through the substitution of marriage for other statuses where marriage equality has been won, or through the impact of 'defense of marriage' legislation in states where that fight was lost, other statuses (including domestic partnership and reciprocal beneficiary) have been disappearing" (Duggan, 2012). Hence, instead of being presented as one option among a variety of familial and conjugal possibilities, marriage has become *the* point of gay liberation, and it has become so to the exclusion of racial, gender, and class equality, and without consideration of how to expand and protect familial and sexual cultures. The one-dimensionality that constitutes the marriage equality movement emanates from the single-issue horizon that this book interrogates. As such, marriage equality is part of a single-issue shift that has helped to narrow the political vision of queer politics. As it concocted marriage as the heart of gay politics, the single-issue turn helped to produce the respectable gay as one of the ideals of neoliberal capital and urbanization, an ideal embodied in whiteness. *One-Dimensional Queer* attempts to reveal the historical contexts for that narrowing and its effects on liberal capitalism, urban space, and state violence.

As a book interested in challenging certain ideological formations that cast queerness as the one-dimensional darling of state and capital, *One-Dimensional Queer* works to place certain alternative critiques within the public domain. Part of that effort involves marking the story of queer liberation as part of a hegemonic struggle – that is, a struggle over how one interpretation has achieved dominance but is in dire need of a critical and historical rebuttal. To this end, chapter 1 presents the Stonewall riots as a major event within the history of intersectionality rather than the history of single-issue insurgencies. This moment of intersectionality includes anti-racist struggles alongside the liberation of queer, trans, and poor people. In an attempt to disinter a subjugated history of multidimensionality, this chapter looks at the intersectional beginnings of gay liberation through the work of queer and trans activists during the late sixties and early seventies. Specifically, Latinx[1] trans activist and Stonewall veteran Sylvia Rivera's retelling of the Stonewall rebellion as the explosive tributary of anti-racist, anti-war, and feminist movements inspires the chapter's entrance into the multidimensional history of gay liberation. The chapter locates this intersectional framing of gay liberation within the ways in which various movements of that era – anti-racist, feminist, queer, and anti-capitalist – were attempting to relate to one another, taking particular note of Rivera and Marsha P. Johnson's creation of Street Transvestite Action Revolutionaries (STAR). The chapter focuses on how queer and trans liberation struggles adopted strategies from the Black Panthers and the Puerto Rican Young Lords, strategies that involved claiming institutional spaces from which people of color, queers, and poor people were excluded. The stakes of this chapter are therefore the intersectional components of queer liberation that were later suppressed by the single-issue focus of gay rights and gay normativity.

Chapter 2 considers how the mainstreaming of homosexuality in the latter part of the seventies and beginning of the eighties took place partly through the gay press and the political as well as cultural backlash to gay liberation movements, a backlash that would express itself with the rise of mainstream gay publications like *The Advocate*. The chapter juxtaposes *The Advocate*'s efforts to separate queerness from new left politics with the explicitly coalitional arguments to be found in the Gay Liberation Front periodical *Come Out!* The chapter offers such pairings as a way to demonstrate how the mainstreaming of queerness through magazines like *The Advocate* represented a move away from locating queer liberation within anti-racist politics and a move toward an ideal of the homosexual as a white and upwardly mobile consumer. The chapter then analyzes how the mainstreaming of homosexuality presumed corporate capital's investment in the creation of gay markets, an investment that was predicated on separating queer politics from anti-racist, anti-poverty, and anti-imperialist movements and interventions. Showing how the mainstreaming of sexuality was an economic and political maneuver, the chapter then connects a one-dimensional interpretation of sexuality as an economic maneuver to the ways in which that interpretation fostered an investment in liberal politics. Part of the chapter's interest in revealing the connections between one-dimensional notions of sexuality and liberal capitalism involves showing capital and state to be entities that have ideological investments in social differences of race, gender, transgender, and sexuality.

While chapter 2 asks how one-dimensional discourses of queerness underpin liberal capitalism, chapter 3 attends to how those discourses undergirded transformations within US cities. More specifically, this chapter examines how the mainstreaming of queerness and the closeting of race have promoted the development of neoliberal urban space. This version of neoliberalization involves the use of queerness as an alibi for an economic and racial cleansing of disfranchised neighborhoods, a move that requires the ideological separation of sexuality from other struggles. Indeed, if single-issue politics have worked to deradicalize homosexuality and separate it from issues of racial, gender, and class justice, then the neoliberal city is the embodiment of that deradicalization. As a result, the chapter looks at gentrifying practices in metropolitan areas as an instance in which queerness helps to define hipness, a hipness that is established by spatially dislocating working-class communities and people of color. While a number of writers have talked about the link between civic planning in and the development of creative industries in metropolitan areas, few have discussed how that link is shaped by discourses about race and the mainstreaming of homosexuality. To see these links one need only consider a quote from US-based Salon.com's interview with the draftsman of the creative class, Richard Florida: "[Cities] must attract the new 'creative class' with hip neighborhoods, an arts scene or a gay friendly atmosphere – or they'll go the way of Detroit" (Dreher, 2002). The quote bespeaks a signature feature of neoliberal urban policy: the construction of creative neighborhoods and cities as tolerant around gayness and anxious about and exclusionary of racial and class differences, a feature that constitutes the mainstreaming of queer cultures, the closeting of race, and the drafting of neoliberal urban policy and the evolution of creative capital. Through the production of safe spaces and the enactment of hate crime legislation that ended up criminalizing the urban poor and people of color, a conception of sexuality divorced from race and class participated in the building of the neoliberal city. Put simply, a hegemonic struggle over the history of queer liberation was also a moment for reproducing urban space away from the forms of gender and familial creativity produced by queers on the margins of race, class, and gender.

In an effort to demonstrate how the single-issue model has legitimated forms of violence, chapter 4 provides a history of how intersectional and multidimensional understandings of queer liberation have tended to see themselves as critiques of violence as a social norm that jeopardizes the lives of people disfranchised by race, gender, sexuality, and class. As such, the chapter uses the critiques of violence coming from intersectional struggles as a way to refuse the narrative of social progress that characterizes one-dimensional discourses. Instead, the chapter argues that it has historically been women of color, queer of color, and trans movements and actors that have illustrated the violence that underpins those narratives of progress.

The book concludes by addressing some of the historical assumptions that attend multidimensional engagements with queer politics. The historical assumptions that it covers have to do with the aliveness of historical alternatives, the need for queer politics to identify and activate those alternatives, the role of queer history as grist for the mill of political theorizing, and the confluence of social struggles as part of the observations of a multidimensional queer politics.

The book is principally interested in the multidimensional beginnings and aspects of queer liberation because of its attempts to create new modes of human existence.

As Tommi Avicolli Mecca argued in the introduction to *Smash the Church, Smash the State! The Early Years of Gay Liberation*, "Beyond the outrageousness, gay liberation was about defining a new form of community and politics for queers, one based on tearing down all boundaries" (Mecca, 2009, p. xi). In this spirit, this book refutes the understanding that multidimensional analyses and activism are examples of a rainbow multiculturalism fitted for the status quo. As this book will demonstrate, multidimensional queer formations helped to produce some of the most powerful critiques of the violences of state and capital and were from their outset attempts to win alternative forms of community and identity.

ONE

The multidimensional beginnings of gay liberation

The Latinx co-founder of Street Transvestite Action Revolutionaries (STAR) and Stonewall rebel Sylvia Rivera remembers the Stonewall riots this way: "All of us were working for so many movements at the time. Everyone was involved with the women's movement, the peace movement, the civil rights movement. We were all radicals. I believe that's what brought it around" (Rivera, 2013a, p. 13). Rivera's memory of the Stonewall riots challenges the taken-for-granted narrative of Stonewall as the origins of a single-issue gay politics. Indeed, in her version of the story, Stonewall is actually made up of drag queens who did not act spontaneously – as the conventional narrative of Stonewall would have it. Neither were the queens politically unseasoned. Rivera suggests that they were in fact tempered in a variety of progressive struggles. Most importantly, Rivera suggests that Stonewall was the tributary for a variety of political movements. As such, her retelling frustrates the notion that Stonewall was a uniform and uncomplicated expression of sexual freedom. Her story demonstrates that rather than existing separately, the movements of liberation from the sixties and seventies were imbricated struggles, not sequential – with gay liberation following civil rights – but contemporaneous, each one attempting (an albeit difficult) conversation with the other. Rivera's argument suggests that what happened on that night was not simply about confining queer and trans liberation to the narrow parameters of single-issue politics, but about connecting that struggle to the network of insurrections that was developing all over the US, a network made up of feminist, anti-capitalist, anti-racist, and anti-war movements.

Part of what the contemporary mainstreaming of queerness does is to obscure the real and historically productive convergences between queer politics and other forms of struggle. This chapter challenges this concealment by pointing to the early affiliations between queer politics and its radical counterparts. The chapter also points to how the past does not represent a moment of deficits and absences where the politics of race, sexuality, class, and gender are concerned, but can be envisioned as a moment ripe with overlaps that are threatened in this current single-issue juncture of dominant gay activism.

Stonewall and the claims of spontaneity

Why is Rivera's retelling important for how we usually tell the story of gay rights? Her version is important precisely because it questions the idea that gay liberation arrived distinct from anti-racist liberation, an idea fostered by the modern gay rights movement. Currently, the modern gay rights narrative is told as a struggle that inherits the successes of the US civil rights movement.[2] Whereas the civil rights movement is framed – under this US narrative – as about race, the gay rights movement frames itself as about sexuality's arrival into the world of rights, as the latest development of freedom after the successes of civil rights. But this version of the story leaves out crucial details. It omits the fact that in several important instances, particularly from 1970 onward, the struggles over race, gender, class, and sexuality were imagined not separately but simultaneously. It fails to mention that efforts at anti-racist and queer liberation have not moved in a linear fashion from bad to better but have moved in many instances in a non-linear fashion that defies narratives of their progressive development. It overlooks the history of how queer and transgender activists from the sixties and seventies drew on a variety of anti-racist movements for inspiration and affiliation, the civil rights movement being only one of them. This version also conceals how queer liberation was not originally conceived in single-issue terms and instead gave birth to a multi-vocal queer politics.

Modern gay rights politics has depended on a certain representation of the transgender women who participated in Stonewall as spontaneous subjects who were seized by an apolitical rage. It was necessary to erase the drag queens as activists prior to Stonewall in order to produce them as pre-political subjects who merely provided a stepping stone to a presumably more mature and single-issue gay rights politics. Rendering them into pre-political subjects was also a way to erase the active dialogue that was taking place in and between movements, and a way to obscure the role that transgender women played in that dialogue. As Rivera's remarks suggest, it is more accurate to say that trans women were the intersectional linchpins between anti-racist, queer, and transgender liberations.

Indeed, the histories of such groups as the Gay Liberation Front, Third World Gay Revolution, STAR, and the Combahee River Collective indicate that movements around queer liberation presumed a whole range of liberatory politics from their very inception and indeed worked to produce a broad and total conception of human emancipation. Stonewall was not the spontaneous "outburst of desperation and vengeance" by transgender versions of Rosa Parks, but like Rosa Parks' actions, theirs were actually the outcome of struggle and political literacy.

Not staying in one's place: the protest at Weinstein Hall

Historian John D'Emilio gestures toward the intersectional meanings of the Stonewall rebellion. When drag queens and other customers at the Stonewall Inn in Greenwich Village fought police who were raiding the bar, that event became – in his words – "the catalytic event that allowed young gay men and lesbians to draw the connection between their own status as homosexuals and the larger political critique that the movements of the 1960s were making about American society" (D'Emilio, 2000, p. 35). As D'Emilio suggests, the Stonewall rebellion was not an event disconnected from the political happenings of the day. Stonewall was a phenomenon that was in dialogue with acts of civil disobedience and protest throughout the country. It was part of the conversation that was produced by the civil rights march from Selma to Montgomery, Alabama, in March of 1965, the picketing of the Miss America Pageant in 1968, and the anti-war march in Washington in November of 1969. As the event that ostensibly inaugurated the modern gay rights movement, the Stonewall rebellion was actually part of a large and multi-faceted dialogue among various groups about the nature and possibility of political insurrection. Contrary to claims about the separatist nature of progressive political formations during the period, groups and activists of all types were in communication with one another about the unfolding and manifold requirements of liberation, a conversation that was inaugurated by anti-racist movements led by the Black Panthers and the Young Lords, in particular. We can see the influence of the anti-racist movements on gay liberation not only in the assertion of anti-racist politics but in movement strategies as well.

In many ways, Street Transvestite Action Revolutionaries (STAR) was the result of an emerging multi-sided understanding of liberation that was shaped by anti-racist and anti-imperialist movements. Indeed, we can see how an emergent gay liberation politics was part of an activist dialogue with other social movements by considering the protest that took place at Weinstein Hall, New York University (NYU), one that occasioned the rise of the group that Sylvia Rivera and African American trans activist Marsha P. Johnson would found.

The group's story begins at the very moment that student activists at NYU were attempting a dialogue with movements outside. Remembering the NYU sit-in as the moment STAR was born, Rivera stated, "STAR was born in 1971 right after a sit-in we had at New York University with the Gay Liberation Front. We took over Weinstein Hall for three days. Members of the larger queer community stepped in" (Rivera, 2013b, p. 52). In the summer of 1970, NYU's Student Government Association allowed the student group Gay Activists Alliance and subsequently the non-student organization the Christopher Street Liberation Day Committee to host gay social functions that involved both gay students and gay members of the communities outside NYU. The events were held at Weinstein Hall, then located at West 11th Street in Greenwich Village, at the time home to the world's largest queer and transgender community. Because of efforts like the ones mounted by the Gay Activists Alliance, NYU was becoming one of the sites for trans and queer community building and organizing. But after two social functions, the NYU administration and board of trustees put an end to any future events, stating that they would not resume until a panel of ministers and psychologists conducted an investigation determining whether homosexuality was "morally responsible" (see Schreiner, 2011). Explaining the context, Rivera goes on to say, "It happened when there had been several dances thrown there, and all of a sudden the plug was pulled because the rich families were offended that queers and dykes were having dances and their impressionable children were going to be harmed" (Rivera, 2013b, p. 52).

After a small initial protest, members of NYU's Gay Student Liberation called for an immediate occupation of Weinstein Hall and requested support from the local Gay Liberation Front. The response was almost immediate, with Weinstein Hall being occupied by dozens of activists, among them Sylvia Rivera and Marsha P. Johnson. On the third day of the strike, riot police raided the hall and ordered the occupiers to leave. And most people did. One viewer described the raid as the "most frightening, naked display of anti-homosexual power" (Murphy, 1971, p. 123). Rivera refused to leave, however, and was dragged out screaming. In a statement about the occupation, she argued, "We would also like to say that what we fought for at Weinstein Hall was lost when we left upon request of the pigs. Chalk one up for the pigs, for they truly are carrying their victory flag" (STAR, 2013, p. 18).

Other protests took place, at Bellevue Hospital where shock treatment was being prescribed for homosexuality, and at the student center where it was still unlawful to hold queer and trans functions (Schreiner, 2011). The protesters generated a list of demands that included the right for queer communities within and outside the university to use university space, open admission for queers and other minorities to NYU, the discussion of homosexuality within university courses, and an end to the psychiatric persecution of queers at Bellevue Hospital.

While the protest at Weinstein Hall was specifically about the presence of queer and trans folks within the university, it is important to note that the inspiration and model for occupying the university so that it could be put to other uses and be liberated from its "proper" uses came from the anti-racist movements. Like Stonewall, the protest at Weinstein Hall bore the imprint of anti-racist politics. Those movements provided the grammar and the politics for seizing and redirecting institutional and political itineraries.

There are several elements that demonstrate how social struggles were in dialogue with one another, elements that prove that protesters were in conversation with other movements as well. This dialogue disrupted the neat divisions between queer, trans, anti-capitalist, anti-racist, and anti-administrative projects. To begin with, STAR arose out of the protests over the administration's regulation of queer life at NYU, a fact that testifies to STAR's involvement and interest in a broad politics that included the immediate and "likely" concerns of transgender folks, and a politics that went beyond the immediate and the likely to issues and places that seemed remote from the needs and circumstances of trans women of color struggling to figure out where the next dollar was coming from.

As Rivera's reference to the parents' and board's objections suggests, the use of Weinstein Hall for queer and trans gatherings disrupted the presumed purity of university space and demonstrated what was to be gained when there might be slippage between the university and the street. While the university administration sought to protect the established programs and itineraries of the university, the protesters at Weinstein Hall insisted on their right to redirect those programs and itineraries. In doing so, they – like other protesters throughout the country at San Francisco State, City College New York, and the University of California San Diego – developed a politics organized around redistributing university space for subjects and practices that previously had no place in and no claim to that space. What was so objectionable about the protests and the activities to parents and administrators was that they were diverting and rerouting the circuits of the university. NYU's Gay Student Alliance and Gay Liberation Front were in effect saying that there are several ways to occupy the space of the university, that the university can be made up of many different types of communities and itineraries – academic circuits, activist circuits, queer circuits, trans circuits, non-white circuits, and so on. As such the protests were about much more than the right of queers and trans folks to hold social functions. They were attempts to produce "other uses for places" that were violently committed to their taken-for-granted uses.

In this way Rivera's lament that the protesters left upon the request of the police is more than a member of the losing side smarting over her and her comrades' defeat by the police. Rivera's refusal to vacate is significant because it represents a refusal to yield to the planned routes of an institution. Her disappointment has to do with the protesters ceding ground to the institution's understanding of itself and the presumably proper practices and people that can be in and represent the institution. The protesters' understanding of the political objectives around institutional spaces is more akin to that articulated by Jacques Rancière denoting a challenge to the "natural order of bodies" in the name of equality (Rancière, 2004, p. 90). This is significant in that Rivera and Johnson become part of an effort to queer and democratize university space. It was one of the earliest instances, perhaps, in which queer and trans folks were attempting to claim the university as an intellectual and institutional space that could not only accommodate but value queer and trans life, value it as part of university community and as the basis of new knowledge within the university. The model for revalorizing minority difference and putting dominant institutions to alternative uses was put in place by the Black Panther Party and the Young Lords.

The protest at NYU was indeed an attempt to intervene in the commonsense meanings of homosexuality – as criminal and incapable of disrupting the status quo existence of institutions like the university. Indeed, the occupation demonstrated queer and trans liberations' efforts to build a politics specifically designed to move out of one's designated place. The takeover at Weinstein Hall represents a refusal of the fable, given to us by Plato, that in order for society to function "everyone" – as Rancière states – "must stay in his proper place" (2004, p. 90).

The difference of anti-separatism

We think of the movements around race, gender, and sexuality as simple assertions of the right of those differences to be respected and recognized. They were certainly that, but the call for respect and recognition was much more than the commonsensical interpretations would suggest. Respecting and recognizing difference in that moment meant an attempt to disrupt the notion that forms of difference can only end up in separation and group antagonism. Indeed, the focus on difference was a way to experiment with modes of difference as forces that could call out to and summon other forms of difference for conversation and coalition. More to the point, those experiments involved taking those differences beyond their assigned and proper places as well and making one mode of difference the occasion for engaging other differences. In the words of Audre Lorde, it was an attempt to challenge a legacy in which "differences have been misnamed and misused in the service of separation and confusion" (2007, p. 115). We can see that summoning in the relationships that developed between groups such as STAR, the Black Panther Party, and the Young Lords. Indeed, the protests and organizing that took place in that moment are a record of the ways in which modes of difference were tested for how they connected rather than separated people.

To begin with, this experiment in connecting and associating various forms of difference could be seen in the Revolutionary People's Convention. The convention was an attempt at making the associations between social differences the norm of radical politics. In 1970, the Black Panther Party sponsored a plenary session in September of that year to plan the November convention. The Panthers sent out this message:

We believe that Black people are not the only group within America that stands in need of a new Constitution. Other oppressed ethnic groups, the youth of America, Women, young men who are slaughtered as cannon fodder in mad, avaricious wars of aggression, our neglected elderly people all have an interest in a new Constitution that will guarantee us a society in which Human Rights are supreme and Justice is assured to every man, woman, and child within its jurisdiction. (Black Panther Party, 1995, p. 271)

The convention would also set the stage for a variety of radical groups to meet and engage one another. Discussing the significance of the convention, Rivera said, "I met [Black Panther leader] Huey Newton at the Peoples' Revolutionary Convention in Philadelphia in 1971 [sic]. Huey decided that we were part of the revolution – that we were revolutionary people" (Rivera, 2013a, p. 13).

In 1970, the New York chapter of the Young Lords Party staged a mass protest against police repression. Like the People's Revolutionary Convention, the protest became the point of convergence of a variety of organizations, ones that represented not only race but gender, transgender, and sexuality as well. Indeed, the members of STAR participated in the protest. According to Rivera, "That was one of the first times the STAR banner was shown in public, where STAR was present as a group. I ended up meeting some of the Young Lords that day. I became one of them." Discussing the relationship between them, Rivera went on to say, "Any time they needed help, I was always there for the Young Lords. It was just the respect they gave us as human beings. They gave us a lot of respect. It was a fabulous feeling for me to be myself – being part of the Young Lords as a drag queen – and my organization [STAR] being part of the Young Lords" (Rivera, 2013a, p. 13). Unfurling the STAR banner at a mass demonstration against police brutality was significant because it showed that activists who might have ceded to a single-issue politics were in fact participating in a wide range of issues and developing a politics that spoke to that range. Developing a ranging and broad-based politics became a point of affiliation for various radical groups.

Creating a broad-based and "intersectional" politics produced real attempts not to privilege one mode of difference over others. To do so meant trying to politicize as many modes of difference as possible. Huey Newton attempted just this in his historic speech on gay liberation and women's liberation in August of 1970. In that speech Newton began by addressing the fact that the radical political climate of the late sixties and early seventies was politicizing various social differences such as gender and sexuality, writing, "During the past few years, strong movements have developed among women and homosexuals seeking their liberation." Newton goes on to say,

> [W]e know that homosexuality is a fact that exists and we must understand it in its purest form: that is, a person should have freedom to use his body in whatever way he wants.
>
> That's not endorsing things in homosexuality that we wouldn't view as revolutionary. But there is nothing to say that a homosexual can not also be a revolutionary. (Newton, 1970)

Newton's speech was an attempt to legitimate homosexuality as a social difference that could be radically politicized. Indeed, he expressed a belief that was operating at that moment: that homosexuality, like differences of race, class, and gender, could be cultivated for its radical potentials.

The politicization of transgender differences was part of that cultivation. Indeed, as an organization built to help transgender women who relied on sex work for survival, STAR was founded as a way to combat the poverty and homelessness that attended living on the street as well as the transphobic violence that came from customers and police officers. Thus STAR attempted to radicalize transgender difference into a social mode that would challenge systemic forms of homophobic and transphobic violence and poverty. As Rivera stated, "STAR was for the street gay people, the street homeless people, and anybody that needed help at that time. Marsha and I had always sneaked people into our rooms. Marsha and I decided to get a building. We were trying to get away from the Mafia's control at the bars" (Rivera, 2013a, p. 13). Nestled in the Bowery, that part of New York that – at the time – was home to homeless straight, queer, and transgender persons, the STAR house was geographically situated in a part of the city where transgender liberation could be united with an anti-poverty politics. Talking about the collaboration, Rivera stated, "Marsha and I decided that it was just time to help each other and help our other kids. We fed people and clothed people. We kept the building going. We went out and hustled the streets. We paid the rent. We didn't want the kids out in the street hustling. They would go out and rip off food" (Rivera, 2013a, p. 13). As STAR's emphasis on anti-poverty and anti-police-violence shows, politicizing transgender modes of social difference meant putting those differences in conversation with other struggles.

The same political climate that occasioned Newton's address and the birth of STAR occasioned other groups and interests committed to broad-based liberatory agendas as well. For instance in the summer of 1970, black and Latino members of the Gay Liberation Front broke away from that organization to form Third World Gay Revolution (TWGR). The group's 16 Point Platform epitomizes that moment's interest in broad-based intersectional politics. Among other things, the 16 Point Platform calls for "the right to self-determination of all Third World and Gay Revolution," "the right to self-determination over the use of our bodies: The right to be gay, anytime, anyplace; The right to free physiological change and modification of sex on demand," "liberation for all women," "free and safe birth control information and devices on demand," "guaranteed income or employment, regardless of sex or sexual preference," and so on (Third World Gay Revolution, 1970c).

Even with all its failures, this period represented one of the most deliberate and dynamic attempts to offer modes of difference as conscious and explicit attempts to produce models of broad-based emancipation. Such a political vision depended on finding ways to put social differences in dialogue with one another, to create contexts for their associations with rather than their segregations from one another. This was very different from the received histories of human emancipation. In the *Communist Manifesto*, for instance, Marx and Engels proposed communism as a revolutionary "movement of the immense majority" (Marx and Engels, 1998, p. 49). Theirs was a movement that based the terms of political emancipation upon the universal ties of labor, ties that would override the differences of its members. Activists in the latter part of the 1970s, on the other hand, were trying to produce political movements that would acknowledge, mobilize, and coordinate the differences of the immense majority.

As this was a moment to experiment with the connections and associations between forms of difference presumed irreconcilably different, it was also the context for developing a politics that refused specialization. Contrary to the presumption that queer liberation stayed neatly in its place, it was in fact moving into various places – that is, into anti-racism, anti-imperialism, transgender liberation, anti-poverty, and so on. In doing so, queer liberation partook of a general characteristic of liberation movements at the time – their refusal to stay put in one political context.

The encounters that social movements toward the end of the sixties were helping to produce provided the political conditions whereby the meaning and dream of liberation were constantly being revised and elaborated. Indeed, one can see that dream, as well as its revision and elaboration, in the history of various activists and organizations. For instance, Asian American queer activist Kiyoshi Kuromiya found his way to activism in the early sixties, working with Students for a Democratic Society and the Congress of Racial Equality (CORE), organizing demonstrations in Maryland and taking part in voter-registration initiatives in the south as part of the civil rights movement. While an early member of the homophile movement, Kuromiya moved away from the single-issue agendas of those movements, later arguing, "The white middle-class outlook of the earlier [homophile] groups, which thought that everything in America would be fine if people only treated homosexuals better, wasn't what we were all about." Indeed, as with other queer activists, the political heterogeneity of the day inspired Kuromiya's interest in expanding radical politics. As he stated, "'We wanted to stand with the poor, with women, with people of color, with the anti-war people, to bring the whole corrupt thing down'" (quoted in Highleyman, 2009, p. 18).

Kuromiya would attend the People's Revolutionary Constitutional Convention. In 1970, Kuromiya would go on to co-found the Philadelphia chapter of the Gay Liberation Front. Kuromiya would see the founding of that chapter as part of the effort to institutionalize a multi-issue politics among queer organizations. Writing in the *Philadelphia Free Press*, he stated, "'We came battle-scarred and angry to topple your sexist, racist, hateful society.'" (quoted in Highleyman, 2009, p. 19). Turning modes of difference into points of connection and association was a way to refuse the specialization that was the norm for political organizing.

The labor power of the non-normative

In Huey Newton's speech about women's and gay liberation, he pondered the idea that "maybe a homosexual could be the most revolutionary." Maybe the statement referred to queer and transgender formations and their potential for radical transformation. Perhaps it referred to groups like STAR and their capacity to cause paradigm shifts in queer organizing in the 1970s. Indeed, if we situate Newton's speech alongside STAR, we come away with a sense that "gay liberation" referred to a host of liberatory struggles targeting poverty, racism, sexism, homophobia, transphobia, and imperialism, pointing to a historical juncture that asserted – in Rivera's words – "that [transgender folks] were revolutionary people" (Rivera, 2013a, p. 13). While anti-racist movements provided other radical groups and activists with a blueprint for revalorizing minority difference and identity and for reshaping institutional spaces and agendas, it was transgender folks who pointed out the influential role that non-normativity might have in radical movements.

To begin with, Rivera suggests that transgender folks offered a kind of revolutionary energy to various political projects. Contrary to the idea that transgender activists played only an initial role in the gay liberation movement or didn't play a role at all in other movements, Rivera suggests that in fact, transgender folks were necessary as they assisted those movements by harnessing non-normativity as a political resource. As she argued, "But in these struggles, in the Civil Rights movement, in the war movement, in the women's movement, we were still outcasts. The only reason they tolerated the transgender community in some of the movements was because we were gung-ho, we were front liners. We didn't take shit from nobody. We had nothing to lose" (Rivera, 2013c, p. 32). The gender non-normativity of transgender radicals worked for the good of movements that were attempting to challenge the presumed naturalness and necessity of the status quo. Rather than their gender non-normativity being an impediment to movement aims and agendas, Rivera suggests that their difference was actually a facilitator of agendas that seemingly bore no explicit relationship to transgender liberation. Put more simply, because the drag queens of Stonewall were denied the presumed privileges of normativity, they could not be seduced by those structures that held out normativity as a reward. In doing so, they illuminated the ways in which non-normativity might be used for revolutionary shifts in the social order, how transgender difference could be a lever that could shift political paradigms and outcomes.

We might locate the coming out – as a critical act – within the political capacities of non-normativity. In a social and political context in which activists experimented with the radical possibilities of differences of race, gender, class, and sexuality, for queer and trans activists, the coming out was part of that radical experiment. For instance, in the inaugural issue of *Come Out!*, the first post-Stonewall publication by queer activists, the editors – members of the Gay Liberation Front – defined the coming out in explicitly political ways: "COME OUT FOR FREEDOM! COME OUT NOW! POWER TO THE PEOPLE! GAY POWER TO GAY PEOPLE! COME OUT OF THE CLOSET BEFORE THE DOOR IS NAILED SHUT!" (Come Out!, 1970a). By using a newspaper to "give voice to the rapidly growing militancy within our community," *Come Out!* demonstrated that coming out of the closet was originally intended to be a way of contesting sexual inequality and producing institutions that could develop forms of contestation. In fact, the magazine saw the coming out as a way to build coalitions with other groups. As the opening page stated, "THROUGH MUTUAL RESPECT, ACTION, AND EDUCATION COME OUT HOPES TO UNIFY BOTH THE HOMOSEXUAL COMMUNITY AND OTHER OPPRESSED GROUPS INTO A COHESIVE BODY OF PEOPLE WHO DO NOT FIND THE ENEMY IN EACH OTHER" (Come Out!, 1970a). Indeed, the magazine showed that "coming out of the closet" was not designed for a reconciliation with the given order, which is how it is understood presently, but as a step toward completely rethinking the given order.

The demoralization of revolutionary consciousness

In addition to the late sixties and seventies being characterized by energetic experiments with social differences of various kinds, the period was also characterized by the demoralization of those experiments and their revolutionary potentials. This demoralization was composed of a series of "isms" and phobias – sexism, racism, homophobia, and transphobia, forces that suggested the social order was impervious to various forms of liberatory change. In its 16 Point Platform, Third World Gay Revolution pointed to the need to break away from the Gay Liberation Front because of the difficulty that queers of color

41

had in relating to the many gay liberation organizations that were emerging at the time, a difficulty that TWGR cited as "due to the inherent racism found in any white group with white leadership and white thinking" (Third World Gay Revolution, 1970a).

In addition to the demoralization caused by racism, there was also the demoralization that resulted from homophobia. In "The Oppressed Shall not Become the Oppressor," Third World Gay Revolution pointed to the effects that homophobia had on revolutionary activities, writing, "By the actions you have taken against your gay brothers and sisters of the third world you who throughout your lives have suffered the torments of social repression, have now placed yourselves in the role of oppressor" (Third World Gay Revolution, 1970b). Identifying the political costs of sexism and homophobia, the group went on to say, "Anti-homosexuality fosters sexual repression, male supremacy, weakness in revolutionary drive, and results in an inaccurate, non-objective political perspective." At the Revolutionary People's Constitutional Convention, a group of self-identified "New York Lesbians" charged the Black Panther Party with sexism as the group recounted details of a meeting in which their demands for "the abolishment of the nuclear family, heterosexual role programming, and patriarchy was called bourgeois" (Come Out!, 1970b).

The demoralization caused by transphobia would also kill STAR. At the 1973 Christopher Street Liberation Day Parade, the (trans)gender divisions within queer communities began to show. Indeed, Rivera remembers that day by saying, "We died in 1973, the fourth anniversary of Stonewall. That's when we were told that we were a threat and an embarrassment to women because lesbians felt offended by our attire, us wearing makeup. It came down to a brutal battle on the stage that year between me and people I considered my comrades and friends" (Rivera, 2013b, p. 53). Finally making it onto the stage and having to negotiate a crowd that was booing her, Rivera shouted, "Y'ALL BETTER QUIET DOWN. I've been trying to get up here all day, for your gay brothers and gay sisters in jail! They're writing me every mutherfuckin' week and ask for your help, and you all don't do a goddamn thing for them" (Rivera, 2013d, p. 30). Rivera said that after she spoke, Lee Brewster, the transgender queen who founded Queens Liberation Front, a group that was active in the 1970s, "got up on the stage, threw off her tiara to the crowd and said, 'Fuck gay liberation'" (Rivera, 2013c, p. 36).

In a 2001 speech, Rivera addressed the restrictions of what has become the current historical juncture organized around gay rights rather than full queer and transgender liberation: "So, what did nice conservative white gay men do? They sell a community that liberated them down the river." Capturing the irony of a normalizing movement born from the militancy of transgender women, she went on to say

> So Stonewall is a great, great foundation. It began the modern day liberation movement, like we spoke before the Daughters of Bilitis and the Mattachine Society. Yes, there were lots of other little groups but you had to be what they called themselves "the normal heterosexuals." They wore suits and ties. One of the first demonstrations that they had, lesbians who'd never even worn dresses were wearing dresses and high heels to show the world that they were normal. Normal? (Rivera, 2013c, p. 35)

As the gay rights movement tells a story in which gay rights starts with a version of the Stonewall riots that forgets the emergence of groups like STAR and Third World Gay Revolution, it in fact elides the ways in which queer politics were emerging as ways to engage anti-poverty and anti-racism. For gay rights to advance an argument of singularity and the uniformity of queer struggles, it had to disappear trans and queer of color activism as linchpins between a variety of political struggles.

The sociologist Emile Durkheim advanced a notion of modern society as moving toward greater complexity. Indeed, that complexity is what we were witnessing in the days that occasioned and followed Stonewall, but one wonders if Durkheim ever imagined those forces within society that made it their business to discipline and restrict that complexity. If the modern gay rights movement is the standard of progress around issues of sexual identity and practice, then progress connotes the narrowing of queer politics. Those are the days that followed.

TWO

Gay emancipation goes to market

In her 2009 essay "Stonewall was a Riot – Now We Need a Revolution," longtime Asian American lesbian activist Merle Woo affirmed Sylvia Rivera's argument that the Stonewall rebellion was a multicultural and multiracial insurgency. Woo wrote, "Stonewall's customers were mostly Black and Puerto Rican, young teenage street queens, dykes and effeminate gays" (Woo, 2009, p. 282). Touching on the significance of that night, she continued, "This was the night that drag queens, transgendered folks, lesbians and gays said NO! No more to gay oppression, police brutality, societal contempt. The homophobia that had oppressed so many for so many years would no longer be tolerated" (Woo, 2009, p. 283). She went on to connect homophobia to the other oppressions that bedeviled folks in the Stonewall Inn and the larger society in general: "Did they say 'No' to racism because they were Black and Puerto Rican? Or 'No' because of their gender or sexual orientation? Was it 'No' because they were poor and working class? It was *all* those things" (Woo, 2009, p. 283). For Woo, Stonewall was not about the triumphant and militant rise of a single-issue politics or identity. It was the night that outsiders "challenged sex-role stereotyping, racism, and class bigotry" (Woo, 2009, p. 283). In her words, "They challenged the dysfunctional monogamous nuclear family, its patriarchal values, oppression of women and children, and sermons that sex is for procreation only" (Woo, 2009, p. 283).

I begin with Woo because of the ways in which she contextualizes the last chapter's discussion of Rivera, Johnson, and STAR's broad political interventions. I also do so to point to how Woo's retelling of the origins of Stonewall suggests an ideological struggle over the meaning and details of Stonewall. In Woo's narrative the details are much more heterogeneous than the dominant narrative suggests. There were African Americans, Puerto Ricans, and lesbians, and in Woo's narrative the social makeup of the people in the Stonewall Inn mattered for the kinds of political demands and visions that made up queer liberation. Indeed, the dominant narrative that has come to define gay liberation is one that occludes how Stonewall was a tributary for a variety of social struggles, not just sexuality. In Woo's account, those social differences did not resolve themselves into a universal and one-dimensional politics that would simply assert sexual liberation to the exclusion of all else.

This chapter considers how this version of the Stonewall rebellion was replaced by a one-dimensional and non-intersectional narrative that depoliticized gay politics. Taking its understanding of depoliticization from a 1966 essay by Stuart Hall in which he defines it as the treatment of a political issue in a "non-political way" (Hall, 2017, p. 89), the chapter considers how gay politics responded to the intersectional potentials of queer liberation by cleaving struggles over sexuality from similar struggles over race, poverty, and gender oppression. As sexuality was depoliticized, it was turned into a "private grouse" (Hall, 2017, p. 95) rather than the inspiration for public redress. Put simply, the contours of depoliticization as it came to shape queer politics emanated from a backlash to the multi-issue character of radical trans and queer politics. This depoliticization did not represent the absence of politics so much as the regulation of politics. As this chapter will show, regulating the multidimensional possibilities of queer politics was part of an effort to make that politics cohere with the political and economic stipulations of liberal capitalism.

The political phenomenon of depoliticization

Three years before the Stonewall rebellion, Hall wrote the essay "Political Commitment," which – among other things – critiqued the use of opinion polls and statistical analyses of voting and election trends as the basis of political strategies. The scholars Sally Davison, David Featherstone, and Bill Schwarz contextualize Hall's piece by writing, "in 1960s Britain the privatisation of politics was already underway and could be named as such. Connected to this was his apprehension that a peculiar quality of the established political system was its capacity to depoliticize politics itself" (Davison, Featherstone, and Schwarz, 2017). Hall described this depoliticization as part of the "end of ideology" (Hall, 2017, p. 87) trend within the sixties, a trend that shunned ideological positions and defined politics as the basis of that rejection. As he put it, "It is … the belief that there is something inherently wrong in seeking ideological models and explanations at all: that modern technological society renders all ideology obsolescent" (Hall, 2017, p. 87). A result of this phenomenon is that ideology and politics are constructed as diametrical opposites: "Within this framework of thinking, ideologies are always described as holistic, millenarian, violent, apocalyptic: whereas politics is practical, pragmatic, middle-ranged, the art of the possible" (Hall, 2017, p. 87). As Hall proposes, the end-of-ideology discourse becomes the reigning narrative of the West: "In some ways, this attempt to drive a wedge between politics and political theory, between piecemeal engineering and social revolution, is the most dynamic ideology we have 'in the west'" (2017, p. 87).

Marcuse had pointed to this very phenomenon in 1964. He wrote in *One-Dimensional Man*, for instance, that technological advances and mass production and distribution had been maneuvered in industrial capitalism against social transformation and critical thinking. About this process, he said, "The most advanced areas of industrial society exhibit throughout these two features: a trend toward consummation of technological rationality, and intensive efforts to contain this trend within the established institutions" (Marcuse, 1991, p. 17). Pointing to the ideological result of this containment, he said the "pattern of one-dimensional thought and behavior" emerges in which "ideas, aspirations, and objectives" are reduced to the given terms of the social order (Marcuse, 1991, p. 12). In their own ways, Marcuse and Hall both pointed to how Western societies were moving toward the narrowing of political universes in the 1960s, reducing politics to the possible and the given.

In addition to reducing politics to the given state of affairs, for Hall depoliticization was also made up of the privatization of the political. As he stated, "I mean the experiencing of issues which are public in character as an unrelated series of private grouses" that culminate in demands that are not articulated "in terms of general expansion and development of community provision … but in a series of structurally disconnected grouses" (Hall, 2017, p. 95). In terms of a political and social situation, this degradation of the political produces a situation in which "the issues fragment, disengage, dissipate. The general discontent becomes sectional discontents, and sectional discontents are by their nature conservative in temper, in that they seek to advance one section against another within the model of the scramble, the affluent free-for-all" (Hall, 2017, p. 96).

Rather than a problem at the level of individuals, depoliticization was seen as a systemic process arising from dominant political and economic orders. As a way of disciplining progressive politics, depoliticization as an ideology worked to confine the political to those standpoints approved by the established systems. Part of depoliticization's maneuvers was to neutralize thinking and actions that tried to transcend the status quo. Neutralizing progressive thinking and action entailed unraveling the potential for politics to produce a constellation of political endeavors. As such, depoliticization denoted the attempt to sever the links between the public and private as well as between one type of struggle and other sets of struggles. Thus, depoliticization denotes the process by which social grievances become private and discrete matters. In a moment of social insurgencies, depoliticization represented a variety of political and economic efforts that were attempting to achieve dominance in the context of those insurgencies.

Gay politics and the beginnings of depoliticization

The seeds for depoliticizing queer politics were sown almost immediately after the Stonewall rebellion. For instance, while Woo, Sylvia Rivera, and others may have narrated Stonewall as the culmination of coalitional struggles, other forces within gay communities would narrate the rebellion in ways that would discredit its coalitional origins. For instance, an article from the *Mattachine Society Newsletter* stated, after describing the bloody aftermath of the fighting between police and drag queens,

> [the] composition of the street action had changed. It was no longer gay frustration being vented upon unsuspecting cops by queens who were partly violent

> but mostly campy. The queens were almost outnumbered by Black Panthers, Yippies, Crazies and young toughs from street gangs all over the city and some from New Jersey. The exploiters had moved in and were using the gay power movement for their own ends. (Teal, 1971, p. 28)

The article frames the entrance of the Black Panthers, Yippies, Crazies, and young toughs as the moment that the rebellion lost its coherence. Rather than people who may have also been invested in gay liberation or queer themselves, the article constructs them as miscreants who were taking advantage of the situation. Indeed, by referring to the Black Panther Party and the Youth International Party (popularly known as the Yippies) as "exploiters," the Mattachine article suggests that the non-queers were interlopers in the struggle for gay liberation and that the heterogeneity of the moment was counterfeit. While the Stonewall rebellion, for Woo, Rivera, and others, was part of a larger ethos of connected struggles for liberation, for the Mattachine article there were no connections to be seen.

In her book *Selling Out: The Gay and Lesbian Movement Goes to Market*, Alexandra Chasin argues that newsletters such as the one from the Mattachine Society helped to produce a thriving homophile movement (Chasin, 2001,

p. 58). Noting the ideological function of the newsletters and the gay and lesbian press, in general, she states, "the gay and lesbian press has played a pivotal role in making gay men and lesbians think of themselves as gay, and as members of the gay community" (Chasin, 2001, p. 58). Moreover, groups such as the Mattachine Society and the Daughters of Bilitis as well as their respective publications "[downplayed] the value of social and collective action" (Chasin, 2001, p. 62), asserting instead the importance of gay respectability. As Chasin states, "These periodicals enjoined readers to observe convention and 'live decently,' in the hopes of proving that homosexuals could be productive members of society, individuals worthy of ... [civil] rights" (Chasin, 2001, p. 63). Echoing this sentiment, the editor of the *Mattachine Review*, Hal Call, argued in 1963, "'To get along, we had to go along. We had to stay in step with the existing mores of society. We had to because we didn't have the strength of tissue paper to defend ourselves'" (quoted in Chasin, 2001, p. 63). Given the pressure to conform to the existing societal norms, it is little wonder that the reporter for the *Mattachine Society Newsletter* would frame the presence of the Panthers and the Young Lords as an exploitative rather than a possibly coalitional outcome.

As an article that interpreted the heterogeneous presence of various progressive communities as the evidence of political illegitimacy, it was also a means of trying to construct queer communities and struggles as separate from other marginalized communities and struggles. In doing so, the article was implicitly contesting the interpretations of Stonewall as a multi-faceted event that exceeded single-issue politics, interpretations that – as Rivera and Woo suggest – were coming from segments within queer communities themselves. We can read the article, seen in this way, as part of a struggle not only over the meaning of queer identity but over queer politics as well. The Mattachine article was hence paradigmatic in that it signaled an increasingly dominant response to the coalitional foundations and possibilities of gay liberation struggles. A discourse would emerge that would associate coalitions and critiques of capitalism from radical queer organizations with expressions of homophobia and totalitarianism, associations that would ostensibly prove the practicality of single-issue politics.

The discrediting of coalitional politics and the crediting of liberal capitalism

In the April–May 1970 issue of the Gay Liberation Front (GLF) periodical *Come Out!*, the University of Toronto Homophile Association wrote a letter to the *Come Out!*

staff. In it, they said, "We are writing to protest against COME OUT!'s attempt to link the homophile movement to communist revolution and support of totalitarian, anti-homosexual political systems." While the letter rightly draws attention to state-sponsored homophobia in socialist countries such as Cuba and Czechoslovakia, it assumes that homophobia is the only option for socialist organizations. About the Black Panthers, for instance, the University of Toronto (U of T) homophile group argued, "Though you claim not to be politically biased the first seven of the nine articles in COME OUT! fulminate against free political and economic institutions and support those (such as the Black Panthers) who advocate authoritarian collectivism at the expense of the legitimate goals of the homophile movement."

The U of T homophiles believed that "legitimate goals" were those in line with the free market systems. As they said, "It is the free market that has enabled state restrictions (and even the results of individual prejudice) against minority groups – Jews, homosexuals, and others – to be as small as they are." If the free market system was the means to regulate social prejudice, then socialism could only be a conveyor for discrimination. Hence, a socialist group such as the Black Panther Party was destined for homophobia, despite the group's unresolved position on homosexuality, as Newton's address on women's and gays' liberation suggested. Associating the group's socialist politics with homophobia, the homophile association wrote in the letter, "It is also a fact that the Black Panther Party terrorists of whom *COME OUT!* is so fond are notoriously anti-homosexual, as a reading of their spokesman, Eldridge Cleaver's book *SOUL ON ICE*, makes very clear." Using the work of Milton Friedman, the neoconservative economist who would go on to be an advisor to both Ronald Reagan and Margaret Thatcher, the U of T homophiles said, "'there is an economic incentive in a free market to separate economic efficiency from other characteristics of the individual."

Similarly, in an article entitled "Gay Power in Pay Power," Leo Louis Martello, former member of the Gay Liberation Front and founding member of the Gay Activists Alliance, wrote, "The love of money is the root of all good." Martello castigates the "have-nothing anti-capitalists" of the GLF for what he perceives to be their idealism: "Do you believe that you're your 'brother's keeper?' If so how do you propose to keep him without money?" Here Martello constructed capital as the most practical way to serve queer communities. In doing so, he also suggested that the potential for social transformation lies in capitalism and that anti-capitalism is the pitiable site of inability (Martello, n.d.).

In the article he references a controversy among the newspapers, an allegation that the June 28th cell of the GLF stole the newspaper *Come Out!* Differentiating the allegedly insolvent and GLF-controlled *Come Out!* from the more financially stable newspapers *Gay Power* and *Gay*, Martello argued, "*Gay Power* and *Gay*, whatever their faults and limitations, are professionally produced publications that pay their writers and their staff. Unlike another publication, they aren't parasites hoping to get everything for nothing" (Martello, n.d.). Martello implied that not only were *Gay Power* and *Gay* run more efficiently but that capital itself was the only real ethical and practical option in challenging inequality. As he stated in the article's conclusion, "How much self-esteem and self-respect can any homosexual have if he has to live on handouts? GAY POWER ... means earning and paying one's way ... Pay Power ... the best way to fight Establishment oppression" (Martello, n.d.). Martello's argument echoes that of the U of T Homophile Association in that it asserted capitalism as the basis of gay liberation. This assertion required gay politics to renounce anti-capitalist groups such as the Black Panthers and the GLF.

What was a simple issue, for Martello, of anti-capitalist magazines mismanaging resources was in fact a structural and ideological issue of those magazines' inability to court advertisers because of their radical politics. As Katherine Sender argues in her book *Business Not Politics: The Making of the Gay Market*, "The explicit critique of capitalism and consumption in radical gay and lesbian feminist magazines was one reason these magazines halted production after relatively short lives, because such a critique precluded the development of sufficiently strong relationships with the more lucrative advertisers" (Sender, 2004, p. 30).

A case in point was the *Los Angeles Advocate*, which began in 1967 as a local political magazine filled with political and tabloid news and was supported mainly by advertisements from "baths, bars, pornographers and bookstores" (Sender, 2004, p. 30). The *Advocate*'s circulation and advertising were due largely to its courtship of advertisers. The magazine would be less known for the issues that *Come Out!* dealt with – that is, issues of capitalism, racism, sexism, transphobia, and consumerism. Because of this the *Advocate* would be able to thrive through supportive advertisers while the other magazines died. Those magazines that were committed to critiques of capitalism and consumption, thus, hit a wall when it came to advertisers who were not committed to those analyses, making the demise of these other magazines not simply a financial matter but also an ideological one.

As Sender contends, the *Advocate*'s transformation in 1974 would only further embed it in a social and ideological context opposed to political and economic analyses. In that year, the wealthy entrepreneur David Goodstein bought the magazine. Goodstein transformed the magazine from a politics and tabloid publication into a lifestyle one. In addition, he would change the name from the *Los Angeles Advocate* to the *Advocate* in an effort to make it more of a national entity. In doing so, Goodstein would, in Sender's words, "reduce [the magazine's] sexual content and [distance] editorials from the more militant factions of the gay civil rights movement" (Sender, 2004, p. 30).

Producing an image of the ideal homosexual was central to Goodstein's effort to distance the *Advocate* from the more radical aspects of the gay liberation movement. For instance, he argued that the ideal gay reader was "male, employed, 'responsible,' having a 'meaningful lifestyle ... an attractive body, nice clothes, and an inviting home" (Sender, 2004, p. 30). Rather than the homosexual being one of the cast of characters in radical struggles, the homosexual would be, for Goodstein, part of a dramatis personae that would pay tribute to what capital might open up for sexual minorities. In this way, Goodstein – like the University of Toronto Homophile Association – was turning Milton Friedman's argument into a dictum: the free market would naturally withdraw from homophobia and help to bring about the freedom that gay radicals wanted but could never practically achieve.

While Goodstein didn't explicitly code his ideal gay man and *Advocate* reader as white, that was undoubtedly the implicit argument. Gay photographer and activist Lionel Biron addressed this in a 1976 article entitled "The *Advocate*: Capitalist Manifesto." Commenting on the *Advocate*'s transformation, Biron wrote, "During the past year the *Advocate* has been transformed into a show place of white, middle class, Gay America" (Biron, 1976). Biron suggests that in order to effect that transformation, Goodstein steered the *Advocate* toward ideological strategies that had been recently put in place by President Richard Nixon: "President Nixon proclaimed himself the spokesman of America's badly maligned 'silent majority.' In 1976 the *Advocate* feels convinced that it can ride the crest of a new gay mandate by scrupulously applying the old Nixonian politics to the Gay Liberation Movement" (Biron, 1976). Biron also argues that part of Nixon's strategy through the discourse of "the silent majority" was to shift attention away from US imperialism: "In the late 1960s Americans were facing an agonizing reappraisal of the U.S. commitment to South Vietnam. Nixon was able to direct the anxiety of many Americans away from themselves towards the anti-war protesters who first revealed that the war was not in the national interest" (Biron, 1976). Hence, part of Nixon's strategy with the "silent majority" entailed moving attention away from the devastation wrought by US imperialism and moving it toward social activism as the real cause of social disorganization within US society.

According to Biron, Goodstein was "attempting to revive the myth of the 'silent majority' for a similar purpose" (Biron, 1976). As Biron contended, "Today, many gays are facing an agonizing reappraisal of their closeted lifestyles. The *Advocate* wants to direct their anxiety away from themselves towards the Lesbian and Gay activists who in recent years have brought gayness out of the depths and into the light" (Biron, 1976). By directing that anxiety away from themselves, white gays could forestall self-reflection and project their anxieties onto activists, thereby constructing leftist activists as threats to gay assimilation. In fact, Goodstein seemed to encourage this othering of activists as threats in an editorial he wrote for the *Advocate*, one in which he stated, "'Gay men and women do not believe achievement of gay civil rights has anything to do with fascism, imperialism, socialism or other aspects of Marxist rhetoric. They are enraged by gay contingents in leftist and "Third World" demonstrations'" (quoted in Biron, 1976).

Here, Goodstein proposes a natural antagonism between the needs and desires of gay liberation and the aims of socialist, anti-racist, and anti-imperialist struggles. In addition to reading Goodstein's comments as a critique of radical publications like *Come Out!*, we might also read them as attempts to forcibly separate international struggles against US empire and class inequality from gay liberation.

Recognizing the ideological and social consequences of this separation, Biron wrote, "This statement is an affront to Black Gays, Chicano Gays, Asian American Gays and all other minority-group gays who must struggle against oppression on more than one front. Obviously, Goodstein would restrict his silent majority to the white middle class which alone can focus on the single issue of gay civil rights" (Biron, 1976). Biron points to how Goodstein and the *Advocate*'s turn to single-issue politics was an attempt to nullify the broad-based coalitions that were initiated in the early 1970s and the impact that those coalitions had on how homosexuality was conceived. Goodstein was attempting to use the *Advocate* to neutralize the ideological transformations that were taking place among queers because of the coalitions between gay, anti-racist, and anti-capitalist liberation. As Biron stated, "The necessity of joining in solidarity with other oppressed peoples, debated so passionately within gay organizations, has raised the consciousness of many white middle class gays, and made us aware of the common roots of class, sexual, and racial oppression and our common goal of human liberation" (Biron, 1976).

The story of the *Advocate* is thus not simply a narrative about a gay magazine's effort to enter the mainstream. It is also a tale of how a capitalist institution was attempting to transform a maligned subculture and social difference into an insignia of capitalism. This transformation was not only about making queerness into something more respectable and palatable for mainstream audiences. It was also about separating gay politics from anti-racist and anti-capitalist radicalism. As such, the market production of the ideal gay was founded on an original opposition to coalitional politics. And inasmuch as transforming homosexuality into a market-worthy entity was a way of producing and capturing a white gay niche market and alienating anti-racist and anti-imperialist concerns, the development of gay capitalism was part of the evolution of racial capitalism, which the black political theorist Cedric Robinson (2000, p. 2) described as "[the] development, organization, and expansion of capitalist society" through racial ideology. The *Advocate* would provide a grammar for developing, organizing, and expanding capitalism through the promotion of gay culture and identity, reformulated to mean the suppression of anti-racist, anti-imperialist, and anti-capitalist politics.

One of the ways that anti-racist, anti-imperialist, and anti-capitalist politics was suppressed and separated from gay liberation was by constructing those politics as *necessarily* homophobic. Indeed, the charge of homophobia became a means of refuting coalitional possibilities between gay, anti-racist, anti-imperialist, and anti-capitalist liberation struggles. The charge of homophobia was absolutely necessary to produce a social order in which gay politics would help to foster rather than contest capitalist and racial inequalities.

The uses of homophobia

Gay liberationists struggled with the reality of homophobia among the left very early on. Indeed, at the November 15, 1969, march on Washington to end the war in Vietnam, Bob Martin, Chair of the Youth Committee for the National American Conference on Homophile Organizations (NACHO), tried to penetrate what must have seemed like an impenetrable political wall among the left by asserting the place of queer liberation in progressive movements. As he stated,

> While the present demonstration is quite properly focused on the injustices perpetrated by the American government in Viet Nam, the ghettoes in the armed forces, in the city of Washington, etc., I think that we should not forget that the same power structure which denies justice in all these areas is doing its best to oppress the homosexually-oriented American. (Martin, 1970)

Martin went on to say that his organization was committed to a coalitional politics and saw the march as an expression of that: "The NACHO Youth Committee has unanimously declared its support for the struggles of the black, the feminist, the Spanish-American, the Indian, the hippie, the young, the student, the worker and other victims of oppression and prejudice." Despite gay liberationists' acts of solidarity, they were often met with rejection from people who should have been allies. Martin continued, "We must note with sadness, however, that many in these oppressed groups have swallowed the whole Establishment's propaganda and have joined in its oppression of those of us who are homosexual or bisexual. We offer our support to you and so often receive but calumny, ridicule, ostracism, degradation in return" (Martin, 1970).

In 1969, Students for a Democratic Society (SDS) organized a project that would mobilize hundreds of young people to travel to Cuba to, in the words of SDS activists Sandra Levinson and Carol Brightman, "'gain direct experience with a Third World socialist revolution and a greater understanding of "revolution" as something that entails much more than guns in the hills, something which means hard work every day'" (Lekus, 2004, p. 57). This project would become known as the Venceremos Brigade. For the gay activists that participated, the Brigade organizers instituted a policy that historian Ian Lekus describes as a "don't ask, don't tell policy that demanded lesbians and gay men not discuss their sexual orientation if they wanted to participate in the work trips" (Lekus, 2004, p. 58). The members of the GLF who participated in the Brigade protested, in *Come Out!*, the homophobia of both the *brigadistas* and the Cuban government. "Gay people," they wrote, "owe allegiance to no nation. The anti-homosexual policy of the Cuban government ... does not simply fail to include gay people in the revolutionary process – it specifically excludes them from that process and the right to self-determination" (Gay Committee of Returned Brigadistas, 1971). To the *brigadistas*, they said, "[We] denounce the national committee of the Venceremos Brigade as the agents of a sexist hierarchy. They, in their liberalism, have not engaged in critical relationship with either the Cuban people or with revolutionaries here" (Gay Committee of Returned Brigadistas, 1971).

While the GLF *brigadistas*, NACHO's Youth Committee, and Third World Gay Revolution believed it was necessary to address homophobia as a problem within leftist organizations and within socialist states, they did not regard homophobia as the necessary condition of anti-racist and anti-capitalist formations. Indeed, they believed homophobia to be a contingent element among the anti-capitalist and anti-racist left. As such, there was the real possibility that anti-racist and anti-capitalist heterosexuals could assume gay liberation as part of their political project as well. Indeed, for many queer activists interested in forming coalitions, Huey Newton's statement in support of women's and gay liberation was proof that this possibility could in fact be realized. The issue of homophobia within the left would become part of a hegemonic struggle over whether it was a matter of contingency or necessity in relation to anti-racist and anti-capitalist organizing. While Third World Gay Revolution, the GLF, and others would argue for the contingent role of homophobia, a powerful response would challenge that assessment and assert that homophobia was part of the essence of anti-racist and anti-capitalist formations.

For instance, in a *Come Out!* op-ed entitled "Questions that Have Never Been Answered to My Satisfaction," an anonymous writer questioned the legitimacy of Angela Davis's arrest and participation in the Communist Party, writing "The Communist Party has been staging demonstrations in behalf of Angela Davis all over the country, and has carefully excluded the banners of groups which support Angela Davis but do not completely support the Communist Party" (Come Out!, 1970c). The writer then continues by suggesting that anti-capitalist agendas are antithetical to queer well-being. As the writer states, "Communist Party members have beaten up members of Gay Liberation Front, in an effort to exclude 'queers' from the picket lines, which the C.P. has been treating as their own private property" (Gay Committee of Returned Brigadistas, 1971).

Another contributor, Steve Gavin, wrote an op-ed entitled "Is Socialism the Answer?" Associating the anti-capitalist left with socialism, Gavin contended, "Some of us in the Gay Liberation Movement have had a rude awakening. Neglecting our own people in the gay community we substituted the 'revolutionary' rhetoric of the sexist left. 'Socialism is the answer,' 'capitalist oppression' are just a few of the phrases used by some to explain our oppression" (Gavin, 1970). The article produces the gay community and the anti-capitalist and anti-imperialist left as diametrically opposed, constructing groups such as the Gay Liberation Front and Third World Gay Revolution as inimical to the true interests of gays. Moreover, Gavin conflates an advocacy of socialist politics with an endorsement of socialist states. As he said, "Perhaps some of us will never come to grips with the notion that Marxism itself may be sexist, that Marxist theorizing like other philosophic theorizing functions as a male chauvinist game, that socialist societies like capitalist societies contain the basic ingredient that is oppressive to gay people – SEXISM" (Gavin, 1970).

GLF representatives responded by arguing against the notion that capital is the protector of minority groups and instead argued that capital is at the root of antagonisms between minority groups: "In a competitive class structure some group must be on the bottom. Hence we are all insecure about losing our position of relative privilege; out of this insecurity comes fear and blind prejudice and the creation of scapegoat groups" (Bedoz, Lewis, and Warshawsky, 1970). After addressing capital's presumed investment in minority liberation, the *Come Out!* staff then challenged the notion that anti-racist groups like the Black Panthers are doomed to a homophobic politics: "We are also painfully aware of the anti-homosexual allusions in Eldridge Cleaver's *Soul on Ice*, concepts we know to be found among some Black Panthers. Here again we say that what leads us to support them and work with them is the understanding of the justice of the cause for which they are fighting" (Bedoz, Lewis, and Warshawsky, 1970). After acknowledging the homophobia at work in the Black Panther Party, the staff members then emphasize that the party is in process on matters of sexuality. They write, "It may interest you to know that we have found individual Black Panthers to embrace us and our cause after we worked, demonstrated, and picketed with them."

Reducing anti-racist struggles to homophobic ones was necessary to disaggregating struggles and to promoting capitalist ideologies. In fact, homophobia as a social discourse profoundly shaped the direction of left political methods – whether toward broad-based intersectional models or toward single-issue ones, and whether toward a critique of capitalism or toward an adoption of it. Homophobia, therefore, was not simply an accident of circumstance where anti-racist and anti-capitalist organizations were concerned. Those groups were by their very nature homophobic.

The issue of left homophobia thus revealed an interest in challenging broad-based political agendas in an effort to assert the political primacy and pragmatism of single-issue and capitalist politics. While homophobia produced tension and likely led to the downfall of coalitions between gay liberationists and other progressives, homophobia also proved a productive and convenient alibi for a turn to single-issue politics. In this instance, homophobia has to be understood as a key ingredient in the comeback of single-issue politics and as part of a hegemonic struggle against a vision of coalitional politics. More specifically, homophobia became code not only for anti-racist and anti-capitalist organizing, specifically, but for any attempt at using gay liberation for coalition building. Homophobia would not then be a simple negative for gay rights but a positive for gay rights (rather than gay liberation) inasmuch as homophobia could be attributed to anti-racism, in particular, and multi-issue politics in general. Homophobia would, contrary to the usual assumptions, be something more than an offense to a social group. It would be a constitutive element in the political discourse of single-issue gay rights, determining who the proper speakers of and the correct politics for gay liberation might be. It would mean that anti-racism, trans liberation, and economic equality would be unviable for gay politics. It would make gay politics conform to interest-based and single-issue politics and usher in the era of gay rights. A singular focus on homosexuality versus a broad politics that could incorporate other urgencies would be understood as the most pragmatic and affirming way for queers to achieve freedom. A single-issue, market-friendly, and politically mainstream gay politics would be a way for queers to rid themselves of necessarily homophobic anti-racist and anti-capitalist leftists. It would also be a way of implicitly asserting a one-dimensional notion of gay community grounded in whiteness and in white consumption. As such, gay politics could be depoliticized away from issues pertaining to poor, trans, and people of color communities – that is, away from the issues that would challenge the workings of racial capitalism. Woo, in her reflections on Goodstein for instance, argued that he used the *Advocate* "to mold a tasteful, moderate image of gays that would be acceptable to non-gay sympathizers within the Democratic Party (the *other* Party of Corporatism)." Molding such an image that would appeal to liberals meant that "[radicals] and militants must be denounced and discredited" (Woo, 2009, p. 286). Hence, a single-issue queer politics would not only provide a racialized ideal of gay culture. It would also narrate gay identity and culture as consistent with liberal capitalism.

From coalitional politics to the politics of liberal capitalism

In the bylaws of the Gay Activists Alliance (GAA), a group that split off from the Gay Liberation Front in 1971, there is a rule that expresses the spirit of single-issue politics. That bylaw states, "The Gay Activists Alliance will not endorse, ally with, or otherwise support any political party, candidate for public office and/or any organization not directly related to the homosexual cause" (Gay Activists Alliance, 1972, p. 5). As an organization that expressed a single-issue orientation, the GAA believed in liberal and legislative reform rather than radical social transformation. Indeed, the GAA would help to set the tone for a single-issue politics of sexuality. Indeed, as historian Terrence Kissack argues, "In the years following the collapse of the Gay Liberation Front, gay politics became increasingly characterized by groups resembling Gay Activists Alliance" (Kissack, 1995, p. 129). In a context in which narrowing queer politics meant aligning sexuality with the mainstream, a way would be opened not only for market forces but for conventional political alliances as well. This alignment would be the entry point for a depoliticized gay politics.

While the GAA set the tone for this depoliticization, the seeds could be seen earlier, indeed during the Stonewall moments. For instance, the Mattachine Society's response to the riots represented an inchoate depoliticization. Describing the Mattachine response, Kissack writes,

Though approached by several people interested in organizing those drawn by the riot, Dick Leitsch, the president of the Mattachine Society of New York, was reluctant to act, fearing that it might damage the Society's relationship with Mayor Lindsay and others whose good graces he had worked hard to cultivate. In fact, the Mattachine Society of New York was uncomfortable with the riots. (Kissack, 1995, p. 110)

The Mattachine response would be paradigmatic of a process of depoliticization in that it would help to usher in a political style appropriate for mainstream political configurations. It tried to establish a "habit of mind" for liberal sexual politics, one that, as the postcolonial scholar Edward Said once put it, "would induce avoidance, that characteristic turning away from a difficult and principled position which you know to be the right one, but which you decide not to take," all in hopes that you will not appear too radical, too controversial to be "balanced, objective, and moderate" (Said, 1994, p. 100). This political style would be explicitly antagonistic to the radicalism of the coalitional elements of gay liberation. More pointedly, the move away from anti-racist, anti-capitalist, and coalitional politics would become the political strategy for those gay organizations trying to enter the political mainstream.

In her discussion of the National Gay Task Force (NGTF) and its move away from countercultural politics, historian Claire Potter argues that one of the early initiatives of the NGTF was aimed at working with the

United States Federal Communication Commission to convince that agency that a partnership between the two groups could work against local and national forms of discrimination "that restricted gay and lesbian economic citizenship" (Potter, 2012, p. 96). NGTF organizers positioned themselves within the Carter administration "through nonconfrontational insider negotiation tactics that pointedly excluded the counter-culture style and community mobilization that were typical in places like San Francisco, tactics that would not be directed at the federal government until the AIDS mobilization of the 1980s" (Potter, 2012, p. 99). Ingratiating themselves with the Carter administration meant depoliticizing queer politics, particularly with regard to race: "Notably, economic and racial inequalities were not publicly advertised themes in discussions intended to normalize gays and lesbians as citizens. Similarly absent from the White House discussions were transgender and transsexual issues" (Potter, 2012, p. 105).

In doing this, NGTF members would distance themselves from the confrontational and grassroots political styles of feminist congressional leaders such as Bella Abzug and Shirley Chisholm. As Potter states, "Rather than deploying the language of class and racial inequality, as feminists did, the NGTF spoke the language of capitalism and the Constitution" (Potter, 2012, p. 106). While both groups – the feminists and the NGTF members – sought entrance into the "benefits of the liberal state" (Potter, 2012, p. 98), as Potter notes, the feminists – more than the members of the NGTF – relied on strategies honed from grassroots movements. As Potter contends, "Feminists who had fought their way to insider status in the party, chose to deploy confrontational tactics to pursue their claims" (Potter, 2012, p. 98). In contrast, Potter argues, "NGTF organizers, many of whom were also feminists, were outsiders who chose to articulate themselves as insiders, both in their style and in a policy strategy that sought to expand the existing claims to recognize their citizenship" (Potter, 2012, p. 98).

Expanding those existing claims meant currying favor with corporate and business sectors. About this, Potter states, "The willingness of the business community to honor gay and lesbian civil rights in the absence of local, state, or federal action, the NGTF argued, meant that the state could ratify changes that already represented consensus among the moderate to conservative opinion makers that Carter would need to push the economic initiatives forward" (Potter, 2012, pp. 106–7). Specifically, NGTF activists emphasized in their conversations with the Carter administration that "government was trailing the desires for nondiscrimination that the private sector had acted upon" (Potter, 2012, p. 107). In doing so, the activists were asserting that the business sector was leading the way in nondiscrimination against lesbians and gays and that it was safe for the federal government to support nondiscrimination (Gay Committee of Returned Brigadistas, 1971). We can locate this strategy of promoting corporate capitalism as the vanguard of gay rights within those struggles between a coalitionally minded liberatory politics and a market-inflected politics. The assertion that gay rights were friendly to capital and therefore friendly with the federal government emerged from the latter.

Summing up the importance of the NGTF in gay politics and the framing of homosexuality as in line with liberal capitalism, Potter summarizes this way: "the NGTF laid a foundation for the reframing of 'the homosexual' as a political, but not necessarily partisan, citizen. This new rights-bearing subject was not actually new, only to be liberated to function in an employment and economic marketplace freed from artificial and invidious distinctions" (Potter, 2012, p. 107). In doing so, the NGTF mobilized the liberal and assimilationist parts of gay politics rather than the anti-racist and anti-capitalist portion of that politics. Thus, the NGTF would also extend the racial, class, and gender exclusions of that assimilationist wing. "NGTF negotiations in the Carter years reveal that the strategy for moving gay and lesbian rights forward was consistent with a homophile past, pushing 'less normal' but more radical and diverse constituencies, like trans people and queers of color, to the margins" (Potter, 2012, p. 108). This strategy would also entail promoting a particular political style: "emphasizing civil rights as having a personal, rather than a public, impact; and achieving incremental goals through a consensus-building process within the state that excited little public attention and required no action by the president" (Potter, 2012, p. 108).

The NGTF's relationship with the US government was, in many ways, an announcement that the depoliticization of gay liberation had found its moment. As it consecrated a politics that was built around the access to power rather than the education and mobilization of the grassroots, it would, as Stuart Hall put it in 1966, "[omit] the praxis of politics" (Hall, 2017, p. 88). With these words he was describing a mode of politics that would eliminate "the whole dynamic by which latent human needs are expressed in political terms and, by being formulated, become the conscious demands of a section of the society, around whom a political agitation can be built, maintained and carried" (Hall, 2017, p. 88). Inasmuch as gay rights politics would push queers of color and trans people to the margins, it would "[omit] the praxis of politics." Instead, gay rights politics would be seen as the ascendancy of a political and economic platform that necessarily meant the suppression of radical coalitions around race, empire, and capitalism. Those coalitions would be described in ways that were consistent with the end-of-ideology ideology – that is, as impractical, foolhardy, homophobic. Not by accident, not by nature, but by design, then, homosexuality would be presented as a depoliticized means of promoting liberal and racial capitalism. In the next chapter we will see how this one-dimensional political style would help to shape urban life and space as well.

THREE

Queerness and the one-dimensional city

The previous chapter considered how queer politics became a one-dimensional affair, how one-dimensionality prevailed in a contest over the meaning of gay liberation, and how it sealed a relationship with capitalism and liberalism. This chapter turns its attention to how a single-issue politics became a part of an urban problematic, perhaps even *the* urban problematic, in which cities have steadily worked to banish their customary denizens – the poor, the communities of color, the immigrants, and marginalized queers who remember the days when queerness was not the sign of respectability and consumption. Queerness would become that, however, through the machinations of city executives and corporate leaders.

In terms of when city officials and corporate heads began taking back the city, the year could have been 1995. In that year New York City Mayor Rudolph Giuliani began leading an effort to redevelop the city and rid it of those stores and theaters that catered to erotic entertainment. That was the year, according to one author (Delany, 1999), when office towers and entertainment centers would go up on each side of 42nd Street. Then again maybe the year was some time after 1984, when New York's Worldwide Plaza was built and more than six theaters were demolished as a consequence. Then again maybe the year was 1975, when police in Philadelphia brutally put down a peaceful protest led by a mostly lesbian of color political organization. It is perhaps more accurate to say that it was all these years and others, for there was no one particular year in which city life narrowed to such an extent that it would cease to accommodate the diverse communities that helped to realize the urban ideal, an ideal that – at this moment – is quickly receding. The point is that in these years queers minoritized by race, class, and gender were fighting with city elites over the meanings and potentials of urban space.

This chapter looks at the ways in which one-dimensional formulations of gay politics helped to give birth to the contemporary neoliberal American city. The chapter attempts to show how this interpretation of gay culture and politics helped to underwrite the ideological conditions that would exclude impoverished queers, queers of color, and trans people from urban spaces that – once upon a time – were their homes. In order to rid cities of communities of color and of the working class, neoliberal urban design fashioned the city as a hub of creativity that was appropriate to the market. In the process, such designs would invalidate the forms of creativity evolved by economically and racially disfranchised queer and trans people, non-normative and insurgent forms of creativity that attempted to produce alternative and in some cases radicalized households and communities. This chapter provides a genealogy of how that happened, how a single-issue notion of queerness would be useful to people who were trying to remake cities into havens of redevelopment, normativity, and gentrification.

The creativity of the gay margins

In *Times Square Red, Times Square Blue* the writer Samuel Delany describes queer life in New York before Giuliani and gentrification came to town. Delany begins by invoking the ethnic, racial, sexual, class, vocational, and religious diversity that characterized New York. Noting the ethnic and racial diversity of Times Square, he wrote, "The population was incredibly heterogenous – white, black, Hispanic, Asian, Indian, Native American, and a variety of Pacific Islanders." Then considering the vocational diversity in the area, he said,

> In the Forty-second Street area's sex theaters specifically, since I started frequenting them in the summer

of 1975, I've met playwrights, carpenters, opera singers, telephone repair men, stockbrokers, guys on welfare, guys with trust funds, guys on crutches, on walkers, in wheelchairs, teachers, warehouse workers, male nurses, fancy chefs, guys who worked at Dunkin Donuts, guys who gave out flyers on street corners, guys who drove garbage trucks, and guys who washed windows on the Empire State Building. (Delany, 1999, p. 15)

Finally, discussing how Times Square and its sex theaters provided encounters between communities typically kept apart, he observed, "As a gentile, I note that this is the only place in a lifetime's New York residency I've had any extended conversation with some of the city's Hasidim" (Delany, 1999, pp. 15–16).

With these observations, Delany describes a sexual diversity that unfolded into diversities of race, class, vocation, and religion, diversities that the theaters facilitated. In doing so, he marks the theaters as institutions that worked in concert with ideals of diversity and engagement across various social identities. Literary and film scholar Dianne Chisholm contextualizes Delany's book in terms of that diversity and the looming threats to it, arguing, "For Delany, as for many others, notably Jane Jacobs, the most urgent problem confronting New York City today, and metropolitan society, in general, is the devastation of inner-city contact space" (Chisholm, 2004, p. 4). Emphasizing Delany's use of Times Square as a metaphor for the city's historic practice of providing spaces of contact, Chisholm invokes a passage in which Delany writes that this is where "'people, male and female, gay and straight, old and young, working class and middle class, Asian and Hispanic, black and other, rural and urban, tourist and indigene, transient and permanent, with their bodily, material, sexual and emotional needs, might discover (and even work to set up) varied and welcoming harbors for landing on our richly variegated urban shore'" (quoted in Chisholm, 2004, p. 4). Chisholm and Delany point to the ways in which a radically democratic conception of the city attempts to promote urban space's potential as a multidimensional site – for creating new possibilities and for meeting needs – that cannot be reduced to the city as the fabled space that will simply satisfy economic uplift. This multidimensional vision of the city regards the urban as much more than the fulfillment of jobs and wealth – rather as the possibility to satisfy desires for self-invention and for the invention of new types of communities.

In many ways, we might say that this multidimensional conception of urban space, one that cannot be reduced to economic imperatives or social conventions, has often been a signature feature of queer engagements with the urban. For instance, during the 1980s New York City's diversity was also characterized by the famous ball houses featured in Jennie Livingston's classic 1990 film *Paris Is Burning*. The houses were institutions built by black and Latinx queers banished from their homes for their non-normative gender and sexual differences. In her article "Queens of Language," the literary scholar Jacqueline Goldsby addressed the houses for how they shaped and reshaped gender identities. As she states, "*Paris Is Burning* bursts open another closet door, leading into New York City's black and Latino drag society, and the culture of Harlem drag balls, where gender-fuck is not just a theoretical concept but is, first and foremost, a way of life" (Goldsby, 1993, p. 108). As Goldsby shows, Livingston's movie shed light on a then underappreciated aspect of black and Latinx life in New York – that is, the ways in which everyday queer and trans people of color were making the city into a capital of gender disruption and re-creation, via communities classed and racialized to the margins.

The houses also made New York into a city noted for its familial experimentation and diversity. For instance, Dorian Corey, one of the veteran trans performers featured in the film, responds to Livingston's request to define the meaning of a house: "'A House? They

are families. You could say that. They are families …
Houses are families for a lot who don't have a family.
It's not a man, a woman, and children, which we grew
up knowing is a family. This is a new meaning of family.
It's a question of a group of human beings in a mutual
bond'" (quoted in Reddy, 1997, p. 370). With her answer,
Corey demonstrates how the houses depart from the
typical heterosexual home partly through their capacity
to encourage gender and sexual identities that diverge
from the gender and sexual conventions and regulations of the heterosexual home. In doing so, the houses
became locations for producing alternative domestic and
familial arrangements. In contrast to the conventional
home, then, the houses were designed around the creative incorporation of black and Latinx queers.

Goldsby connects this creativity to the exclusion that
these queers of color faced in the homes in which they
grew up, arguing, "Establishing a stable life is a prior-
ity for the gay men, transvestites, and transsexuals who
are citizens of the ball world" (Goldsby, 1993, p. 108).
Identifying the specific urban spaces that became the sites
for gender and sexual recreation, Goldsby adds, "Dis-
owned by their families of origin because of their sexual
orientations, the 'children' (the terms house members
use to refer to themselves) flock to the piers fronting the
Hudson River near Christopher Street where, as Cherie

Moraga would say, they 'make *familia* from scratch,' finding safer refuge in cliques or family units known as 'houses'" (Goldsby, 1993, p. 108). As Goldsby suggests, the exclusion from the domestic and private space of the heterosexual home would inspire queers and trans people of color within New York to claim such public venues as the piers that looked onto the Hudson River. In this sense, those queer and trans folks were designating such public spaces as sites of gender and sexual reinvention as well. Elaborating on this use of public spaces, Chandan Reddy argues, "the film … is set to visual shots not of any of the subjects' homes, but of queer of color 'counter-publics' such as the Christopher Street Pier and the small parks that dot Greenwich Village" (Reddy, 1997, p. 371), a fact that makes the houses that those folks created "non-identical" to the heterosexual home inasmuch as the reinvention of gender and sexual identities of the houses are connected to the reinvention of public space.

Writing about New York queer life in the 1990s, anthropologist Martin Manalansan noted the ways in which immigrant and people of color communities contained spaces for gender and sexual diversity as well. In his book *Global Divas: Filipino Gay Men in the Diaspora*, Manalansan tells the story of a bar in Queens "located in the Latino neighborhood of Jackson Heights and a block away from the elevated tracks of the no. 7 train" (Manalansan, 2003, p. 71). The bar is one in which "the clientele, staff, and music are primarily straight until 7p.m., after which everything changes" (Manalansan, 2003, p. 71). Describing that change, he writes,

> from the people drinking to the ones serving the drinks to the music played, it becomes a gay bar ... And at 7:01 P.M., the new bartender stepped in, placed a tape in the stereo system, and started playing a dance song by Madonna. Soon, several men arrived; some, at least to us three Filipino observers, seemed gay or as one of my companions said, "queenly." (Manalansan, 2003, p. 71)

Rather than the image of an always already homophobic neighborhood of color, Manalansan provides a glimpse into the complicated relationship that those neighborhoods have with queer sexuality.

In his article "'That's My Place!': Negotiating Racial, Sexual, and Gender Politics in San Francisco's Gay Latino Alliance, 1975–1983" the late Latinx Studies scholar Horacio N. Roque Ramírez cites San Francisco's Latino Mission District as an urban space that during the seventies and eighties made itself available for queer of color creativity and reinvention. Referring to the queer Latinx immigrants and American citizens who left their nations, regions, homes, and families for "radically new opportunities for queer collective belonging" (Roque Ramírez, 2003, p. 225), he writes, "Sexiles landing in the Bay Area met thousands of individuals who by birth or life experience had always considered the region and, in particular, San Francisco's Latino Mission District as their home ... Whether homegrown or sexiled, these 1970s gay Latino activists were less interested in 'transcending' differences than in incorporating the multiple dimensions of their social experience" (Roque Ramírez, 2003, p. 225). Rebutting the white queer author Armistead Maupin's claim that San Francisco allowed queers to "'[transcend] the usual boundaries of race, class, and region'" (quoted in Roque Ramírez, 2003, p. 226), Roque Ramírez suggests that the migration of Latinx queers to the Bay Area transformed urban space in such a way that particularities of race, gender, sexuality, class, and culture could commingle, producing new encounters, identities, and communities.

As an example of the ways in which the Gay Latino Alliance (GALA) attempted to make the Latinx space of the Mission District one that spoke to the needs and interests of Latinx gays, Roque Ramírez offers these remarks from Diane Felix, a founding Chicana member of the organization: "'GALA was founded in 1975 in San Francisco in response to a need for an organization that would struggle for the rights of lesbian and gay latinos'" (quoted in Roque Ramírez, 2003, p. 239). Expounding on that need, Felix goes on to say, "'We saw many Latinos driven into a Gay subculture where they were victimized by racism, sexism, and cultural alienation'" (quoted in Roque Ramírez, 2003, p. 239). Attempting to promote a multidimensional understanding of Latinx and gay identities, the group participated in San Francisco's Gay Freedom Day Parade, its celebrations for Cinco de Mayo, and the city's Carnaval Festivals, oftentimes carrying politicized placards with slogans such as "'Gay Latinos Against Somoza,' 'Support Affirmative Action,' 'End Racism,' 'Puerto Rico Libre,' 'E.R.A. [Equal Rights Amendment] Now'" (Roque Ramírez, 2003, p. 240). Pointing to the ways in which the organization's political commitments were interwoven with its social ones, Roque Ramírez argues, "While GALA's public statements called for political change locally and internationally, it was the prominent live salsa *orquestras* or bands that kept hundreds of women's and men's bodies dancing in the nighttime merriment. Politics and dancing mutually supported one another; the funds GALA raised through the dances and other social events underwrote political activism" (Roque Ramírez, 2003, p. 241). As an organization that was using the Mission District to articulate a multidimensional queer politics and produce forms of Latinx community that exceeded heterosexist norms, GALA claimed urban space in ways that would exceed narrow political and economic interests.

Another organization that attempted a similar social and political engagement was the Philadelphia-based DYKETACTICS! In her description of Philadelphia in the 1970s, former member and gender studies scholar Paola Bacchetta writes about the racially and ethnically diverse lesbian political group, saying, "Most of us had come from and remained within other movements: for national liberation, Black liberation and civil rights, anarchist and socialist movements, and so on" (Bacchetta, 2009, p. 218). Bacchetta identifies the multidimensional and intersectional politics of the group, writing, "As a group we saw our liberation as inseparably encompassing struggles against lesbophobia, sexism, racism, poverty, neocolonialism, capitalism, and the destruction of the environment" (Bacchetta, 2009, p. 218).

In terms of the group's impact on neighborhood and urban space, DYKETACTICS! organized "a citywide women's general strike to protest working women's double work day, unequal pay and high rates of unemployment" (Bacchetta, 2009, p. 222). In addition, they "issued statements in solidarity with SEPTA (SouthEast Pennsylvania Transport Authority) workers striking for better pay and working conditions" (Bacchetta, 2009, p. 222). After encountering police violence because of their activism, they also filed a federal lawsuit against the Philadelphia police for brutality against lesbians, becoming the first lesbian group in the US to do so. Within their home, the group also worked to produce a woman-affirming and non-hierarchical space organized around collective living and cooperation.

Against the city's Bicentennial Celebration of the Declaration of Independence in 1976, the group wrote their own "Lesbian Feminist Declaration of 1976." In it, they stated, "The American nation has been founded on the genocide of Native American peoples, financed through the slavery of African and Third World peoples and sustained through the oppression of all women. All of these atrocities have been sanctioned by men's religions" (Bacchetta, 2009, p. 227). Addressing US geopolitics, the Declaration went on to state, "'He [the Man] develops a global system of imperialism which enslaves much of humanity and threatens the entire world. Under the guise of making the world 'safe for democracy,' he imposes his culture, his government and his religions on other nations. He steals their human resources to make the United States the richest land on earth'" (Bacchetta, 2009, p. 228). The group posted copies of the Declaration on the gates outside the mansion of the Archbishop of the Archdiocese of Philadelphia, read the Declaration to the congregants of the First Presbyterian Church in one of the elite suburbs outside of Philadelphia, and went to another wealthy suburb and read the Declaration to the St. George's Episcopal Church's congregation (Bacchetta, 2009, p. 228). With these actions, the group demonstrated that the city was the location in which a series of anti-capitalist, anti-racist, feminist, and queer encounters could and should take place.

Queers in cities such as New York, Los Angeles, Philadelphia, and San Francisco claimed urban space in the seventies and eighties as a way to produce multidimensional conceptions of queer sexuality, conceptions that promoted overlaps between sexual, racial, gender, and class identities. In doing so, they presented communities of color as contradictory spaces, ones that were not only characterized by homophobia but also disposed to the creation of radical queer formations. The spaces that radical queers created were also multidimensional in the sense that they attempted to meet needs that could not be reduced to the single-issue ideals and concerns of market imperatives or of normative familial and domestic arrangements. Rather than see the city as the space to reproduce normativity or simply to satisfy wage labor or capitalist production, minoritized queers were trying to engage the city as the site for the invention of new kinds of households, communities, families, identities, and politics. The claims that they made upon the city as the domain for reinvention and community would challenge the hegemony of political and economic leaders. Little wonder, then, that the people's claim on the city would be a primary target of the city's leaders.

Redevelopment and repression

Delany's *Times Square Red, Times Square Blue* provides a warning about the political and economic projects that were trying to suppress the multidimensional creativity of queer subjects. Talking about the ways that Times Square was changing under the city's plans for redevelopment, Chisholm invokes Delany again, writing:

> New Times Square represents a "safe," upper-middle-class space from which heterogeneous commingling and (homo)sexual loitering, along with the sex shops, porn cinemas, and peep shows, will be systematically removed and/or relocated, thus converting lively gay space into a dead straight zone, a zone of official business by day and a wasteland after dark. It is not the demolition of decay but the targeting of "decadence" that alarms Delany, and that promises to be "disastrous" to gay society and social diversity. (Chisholm, 2004, p. 4)

As the passage implies, the city's plans for redevelopment would stamp a heterosexist and elitist ideology on urban space, one that would be a way of cleansing the city of its queer character and possibilities. As an ideological (rather than purely economic) venture, urban redevelopment would demonstrate the ways in which the city's plans for renewal were constituted by discourses of sexuality, class, and race. This multidimensional queer character is the "decadence" that the city is attempting to destroy, the decadence that represents the satisfaction of desires that cannot be reduced to the economic, racial, and heterosexual imperatives of the city.

In such a context, queers marginalized by race and class become the witnesses to city government's destruction of the possibilities for a multidimensional life. Relating the Marxist theorist Walter Benjamin's work to Delany's writings, Chisholm states, "With Benjamin, Delany shares an emphasis on the erotic as the terrain and perspective from which to recast the shock of urbanization and to reveal changes most powerfully wrought upon the human sensorium" (Chisholm, 2004, p. 6). The erotic becomes in this context not simply an expression of sexual desire but the vantage point from which to observe all that would be lost as the city's leaders attempted to rid New York of its queer excesses, "excesses" that really amounted to the chance for everyday people to reinvent themselves and their communities.

In order to cleanse New York of those excesses, the Giuliani administration activated the city's repressive apparatuses. More specifically, one of the ways that the Giuliani government enforced redevelopment was through the use of the city's police forces to guarantee its "quality of life" campaign. Noting the ways that this campaign impacted queer spaces, Manalansan writes, "Mayor Rudolph Giuliani promulgated a 'quality of life' campaign that virtually wiped out public queer spaces in many areas of the city." The redevelopment and quality of life project was one in which the city's economic redevelopment was assisted by police repression and violence. Manalansan says this about repression taking place at the time: "In a city marked by overlapping and contradictory sites, New York City queer of color spaces are oftentimes circumscribed by larger forces such as federal, city, and state laws. During my fieldwork from the early to late 1990s, the New York City police were accused of harassment and cruelty against people of color" (Manalansan, 2003, p. 88).

Describing one informant's story, Manalansan writes, "One of my informants was arrested once, and he spent two nights in jail. He said he was a victim of entrapment; the policeman who arrested him kept talking about the

INS [Immigration and Naturalization Service] and deportation rather than jail. My informant was terrified because he was here on a work visa and could be easily sent back to the Philippines" (Manalansan, 2003, pp. 80–1). The city's redevelopment, therefore, required preying on the specific vulnerabilities of diverse communities made up of people of color, the poor, and immigrants.

While the redevelopment campaign would attempt to rid the city of people of color, queers of color, and poor people, that population would be needed as laborers for the newly redeveloped city. As Manalansan states, "The gleaming modernity of New York City's financial, commercial, and cultural centers with highly educated, mostly white personnel is supported by a gendered, ethnicized, and racialized substratum" (Manalansan, 2003, p. 64). This substratum would thus be reduced to what the city's political and economic leaders had in mind all along: workers who would satisfy nothing more than the city's economic and ideological needs. Stated differently, New York capital's growth and development helped to foster the conditions for the violent repression and expulsion of queers of color, people of color, and poor people. The violence of this repression would be shaped by the imperative to reduce the multidimensional creativity of marginalized people to a single-issue existence as wage laborers. In particular, the redevelopment project was a way of saying to marginalized communities that New York and cities in general were not theirs to create alternative identities, practices, or communities.

Neoliberal affirmation, repression, and the city

One of the ways that city leaders managed to banish marginalized communities in general, and racially and economically disfranchised queer communities in particular, is through efforts to produce "the creative class." As urban geographer Jamie Peck has argued, Richard Florida has, since the 2002 publication of his influential *The Rise of the Creative Class*, become the guru for city officials around the world seeking to attract "creative talent." As Peck says,

> From Singapore to London, Dublin to Auckland, Memphis to Amsterdam; indeed, all the way to Providence, RI and Green Bay, WI, cities have paid handsomely to hear about the new credo of creativity, to learn how to attract and nurture creative workers, and to evaluate the latest "hipsterization strategies" of established creative capitals like Austin, TX or wannabes like Tampa Bay, FL: "civic leaders are seizing on the argument that they need to compete not with the plain old tax breaks and redevelopment schemes, but

on the playing fields of what Florida calls 'the three T's [of] Technology, Talent, and Tolerance.'" (Peck, 2005, p. 740, quoting Shea, 2004)

Florida's creative city plan was not only a way to make way for elite classes, it was also a way of channeling queer creativity for the good of the market, as well as a means of evicting the forms of queer creativity that exceeded and critiqued market capitalism. Florida's creative class, therefore, represents not so much the ascendancy of the best and the brightest but the will to dominance of people who will harness creativity for economic might.

To begin with, Florida identifies diversity as a necessary factor for attracting members of the creative class to a company located in an urban area. Discussing the significance of diversity for urban areas, he writes, "Diversity is favored first of all out of self-interest: it can be a signal of meritocratic norms" (Florida, 2012, p. 57). Discussing how prospective employees use diversity as a measure of meritocratic cultures within a company, he states, "A number of creative class people have told me that they always ask if a company offers same-sex partner benefits when they are interviewing for a job, even if they are not gay themselves. What they're seeking is an environment that is open to differences – of gender, sexual preference, race, or even personal idiosyncrasies"

(Florida, 2012, pp. 57–8). In this context, queerness in the form of same-sex partner benefits becomes a proxy for a company's respect for diversity. Hence, a company's investment in a particular and narrow expression of queer intimacy – the couple form – becomes a sign of that company's moral virtue.

Discussing the presumed correlation between queerness and its relationship to the economic prospects of cities through what he calls "The Gay Index," Florida argues, "[We] see a strong and vibrant gay community as a solid leading indicator of a place that is open to many different kinds of people" (Florida, 2012, p. 238). Continuing to read queerness as a proxy for all types of diversity, he continues, "If gays feel comfortable in a place, then immigrants and ethnic minorities probably will, too, not to mention eggheads, eccentrics, and all other non-white-bread types who are the sources of new ideas. As Bill Bishop [author of 2008 *The Big Sort: Why the Clustering of Like-Minded America is Tearing Us Apart*] put it, 'Where gay households abound, geeks follow'" (Florida, 2012, p. 238). In Florida's formulation, queerness becomes a mode of difference that can promote capital's well-being. Thus, he attempts to align queerness with market needs and imperatives.

Indeed, in her book *Safe Space: Gay Neighborhood History and the Politics of Violence*, historian and American

Studies scholar Christina Hanhardt contextualizes Florida's index by arguing, "The Gay Index, based in the research of demographer Gary Gates, was, by the start of the 2000s, a measure celebrated by city agencies from Washington, D.C. to Oakland, California, because it was highly touted as predictive of the regional success of high-tech industries" (Hanhardt, 2013, p. 186). Hanhardt continues by saying, "In this formulation, gay space is, thus, an index of economic competitiveness in a global marketplace for business location" (Hanhardt, 2013, p. 186). We might understand this use of queerness as hailing from the efforts of activists and entrepreneurs such as Leo Louis Martello and David Goodstein to make queerness a helpmate to rather than an adversary of capitalist economic formations.

While Florida's index ostensibly promotes an undifferentiated gay, that gay's ability to attract economic value presumes certain class and racial particularities. We can better detect that particularity in what he says about the impact of queerness on housing values. Florida states, "It really wasn't such a leap – urbanists have long recognized that gentrification (and the higher housing prices that follow) is set in motion by creatives, artists, and gays" (Florida, 2012, p. 243). Discussing statistical measures that could presumably determine how certain variables affect housing values, he goes on to say, "The second and much larger factor is reflected by the combined Bohemian-Gay Index which merges the concentration of artists, musicians, and designers with the concentration of gays and lesbians in a region" (Florida, 2012, p. 244). Discussing the similar impacts that "bohemians" and "gays" have on housing values, he argues, "Regardless of which variables we applied, what version of the model we used, or which regions we looked at, the concentration of bohemians and gays consistently had a substantial correlation with housing values, even after controlling for income, human capital, jobs, and city size" (Florida, 2012, p. 244).

Noting the racial particularities of Florida's "gays," Hanhardt writes, "Although for Florida acceptance of gays represents the far reaches of tolerance and diversity, his curious definition of the latter is absent people of color. As Florida observes when describing the Composite Diversity Index of which the Gay Index is a part ..., 'the diversity picture does not include African Americans and other minorities'" (Hanhardt, 2013, p. 187). Indeed, as Florida himself acknowledges, "'My research identifies a troubling negative statistical correlation between concentrations of high-tech firms and the percentage of the non-white population'" (quoted in Hanhardt, 2013, p. 187).

Florida makes this argument about the positive value that being gay has on housing values within the context of a housing market that is structurally racist toward black and Latinx people. Historically, the US housing market has regarded racially and ethnically underrepresented groups as negative factors for housing values, buttressing racist discourses that constitute those groups as liabilities for property values within a community. Moreover, Florida's index separates "gay" from "immigrants" and "ethnic minorities." In doing so, his index cannot account for the differential values that may be assigned to immigrant queers and queers of color, that their value in the housing and economic market will not be the same as that of white gays. As such, Florida's index reveals itself as not so much a general gay index but an index of the value that white gays bring to the market.

Florida's creative city design is, thus, based on a model that abstracts race and class from the category "gay." In this, he has propagated a one-dimensional model of queerness as the basis of urban and economic renewal around the globe. As such, the gay index selectively incorporates certain forms of queerness into regimes of respectability and economic valorization. Discussing the consequences of this selective incorporation, Grace Hong argues, "Access (or lack thereof) to gendered and sexual respectability becomes the dividing line between those who are rendered deviant, immoral, and thus precarious and those whose value to capital has been secured through a variety of forms" (Hong, 2015, pp. 19–20). Read through Hong's arguments, Florida's Gay Index becomes a way of producing certain forms of queerness – those with access to racial and economic privilege – as the antithesis of those forms produced as deviant, immoral, and precarious. There is a direct relationship between valorizing economically white queers and criminalizing trans, queer of color, poor and working-class queers, and immigrant queers, a criminalization that justifies their expulsion from urban space. As trans studies scholar Jin Haritaworn suggests, indices like Florida's render people of color communities disposable "on account of both their 'inferior and deficient' cultural values and their decreased labour value in a post-Fordist regime of capital flight and restructuring" (Haritaworn, 2015, p. 6). Redevelopment, then, has to be seen as a mode of violence rather than a general good for racial, ethnic, gender, and sexual minorities.

In addition to deploying a selective notion of gay, Florida's plan also produces a selective notion of creativity. If creativity during the sixties, seventies, eighties, and nineties among marginalized queer communities and subjects meant the creation of alternative forms of family, intimacy, and domesticity, then Florida's plan was designed to channel creativity for the good of economic life rather than the multidimensional good of queers in all their gender, sexual, racial, ethnic, and class varieties. In this sense Florida's plan encourages city planners and municipal officials to narrow queer creativity as much as possible to the needs, desires, and interests of the market, making the role of those planners and officials the alignment of queerness with neoliberal structures. Discussing the role of neoliberalism in government, Jodi Melamed argues, "Neoliberal rationality induces governments to think and act nongovernmentally, that is as businesses whose business is to engineer and manage human, organizational, legal and natural resources to maximize value and optimize productivity" (Melamed, 2011, p. 147). Florida's index, we might say, is designed to engineer and manage queer resources to maximize and optimize economic productivity, a maximization and optimization that have led to the expulsion of disfranchised people to the outskirts of city life. Melamed captures the violence of this aspect of neoliberalism when she contends, "Neoliberalism becomes recognizable as a mode of rationalizing biological and social life when we attend to the violence it inflicts upon human beings and communities in the name of economic restructuring" (Melamed, 2011, p. 147). As the case of New York implies, the violence of neoliberalism was inflicted on queers of color and people of color through their exploitation as workers within the city, their expulsion from the city, and their criminalization by the city.

Neoliberalism and the suppression of queer powers

In Robert E. Park, Ernest Burgess, and Roderick D. McKenzie's 1925 book *The City*, Park argued this about "the city plan" as a way of making and shaping cities: "It is because the city has a life quite its own that there is a limit to the arbitrary modifications which it is possible to make (1) in its physical structure and (2) in its moral order" (Park, Burgess, and McKenzie, 1967, p. 4). Explaining the ways in which the plan for a city is limited by the "life" of the city, Park went on to say, "The city plan, for example, establishes metes and bounds, fixes in a general way the location and character of the city's constructions, and imposes an orderly arrangement, within the city area, upon the buildings which are erected by private initiative as well as by public authority" (Park, Burgess, and McKenzie, 1967, p. 4). For Park, it is the life of the people who actually live within a city that tempers the might and power of the city plan. As he states, "Within the limitations prescribed, however, the inevitable processes of human nature proceed to give these regions and these buildings a character which it is less likely to control" (Park, Burgess, and McKenzie, 1967, pp. 4–5).

The story of neoliberal redevelopment is one in which city planners have attempted to gain power over the ability of the city's inhabitants to shape the "character" of urban space. Inasmuch as gentrification and redevelopment efforts were designed to clean the city of communities characterized by their non-white, immigrant, and non-normative constituencies, city planners were attempting to usurp control from marginalized residents to shape the character of urban spaces. Moreover, to the extent that Florida's creative city plan was aimed at directing the creativity of queer inhabitants toward the needs and interests of the city's political and economic elite, the city planners were attempting to override the limitations that everyday people imposed on those planners. In this way the neoliberal project as it pertains to cities is to make one-dimensionality – the use of the people's resources, labor, and creativity for the good of the city's economic prowess and its elite – the law of the land.

Pointing to the antagonism between corporate leaders and New York City's minorities, geographer David Harvey discusses how capital responded to the stabilization and recovery programs put in place by New York City government during the sixties and seventies, programs that attempted to integrate "racial minorities into the labour force through public employment" (Harvey, 2007, p. 6). In that context, New York City's investment bankers decided not to lend more monies to the city. Harvey writes, "Clearly New York City was vulnerable, what was New York City doing that the investment bankers didn't like? What they were doing was playing nice to the unions, they were actually spreading the money around, and they were engaging in all kinds of philanthropic projects, actually being nice to minorities, black people and all the rest of it" (Harvey, 2007, p. 7). Pointing to how the city's overtures toward blacks, the poor, and working people ran foul of investor interests, Harvey goes on to say,

> The city was doing all kinds of things that stood in the way of the ambitions of men like David Rockefeller who wanted New York to be an island of bourgeois affluence. At the same time that the monies were being pushed, there was a lot of anti-banker sentiment in the city and a lot of anti-corporate sentiment in the city. (Harvey, 2007, p. 7)

New York capitalists' response exemplifies the ways in which capitalist elites were in fact trying to regain authority over labor unions and the communities that had become empowered via the expansion of the public sector.

To the extent that corporate and city officials were interested in ridding the city of those populations who generated a critique of state and capital and also produced forms of family and domesticity that exceeded the nuclear family model, those populations had to be brought in line with interests like those of Rockefeller, interests that attempted to remake the city into a haven of "bourgeois affluence." As Hanhardt argues, "Neoliberalism not only transformed the structure of accumulation under capitalism, but it – along with the attendant growth of financialization – also reshaped the ideologies of everyday life to naturalize the market and downplay group inequality" (Hanhardt, 2013, pp. 22–3). Naturalizing the market has been a project of racial capitalism. As Hanhardt states, "Neoliberalism has reshaped cities like New York and San Francisco in ways that foster hypersegregation and exploitation: the privatization of public services, corporate tax breaks, attacks on tenant protections, the expiration of mandates for low- and middle-income housing, public subsidies for private-market value construction, and the mass expansion of security forces are but a few of its policies" (Hanhardt, 2013, pp. 187–8). Redevelopment or making the city into a "haven of bourgeois affluence" connoted the naturalization of the market and the downplaying of social inequalities, processes that account for the alienation that embeds redevelopment. As a result, the story of redevelopment is one of how people have been forcibly and violently alienated from producing the city that they want, the city that would meet their needs, and the city that would accommodate their desires to be more than what government and capital dictated.

Extending the notion that the city is a site for wrestling with the possibilities of human achievement, Harvey argues that the building of a city is always a way of proposing a certain vision of community. To that end, he argues this about the great cities of the world – New York, Moscow, Shanghai, Toronto, and Birmingham: "the result of that kind of urbanization has been the creation of a certain kind of human society, and we have to pay attention to the kind of human society this is" (Harvey, 2007, p. 3). With regard to neoliberalism's vision of human community, he writes, "neoliberalization, from its very inception, was about the restoration of class power and, in particular, the restoration of class power to a privileged elite, i.e. the investment bankers and top corporate chiefs" (Harvey, 2007, p. 12). Given that this chapter has attempted to illustrate the ways in which neoliberalization was a way to exclude and manage the labor and creativity of communities marginalized by their racial, gender, and sexual differences, neoliberalization has also connoted the restoration of power for an elite characterized by their access to normative privileges of gender, sexuality, and race.

In his discussion of Friedrich Engels's 1845 text *The Condition of the Working Class in England*, the theorist Henri Lefebvre wrote this about Engels's discovery of contradictions between great wealth concentration and massive power, and between the awe-inspiring beauty and dispiriting ugliness of urban societies: "this prodigious social wealth, which came to fruition under the economic and political control of the English bourgeoisie, was accompanied by sacrifice. Londoners 'have been forced to sacrifice the best qualities of their human nature to bring to pass all the marvels of civilization which crowd their city'" (Lefebvre, 2016, p. 7, quoting Engels). Drawing out the consequences for the working masses of building the city's wealth and beauty, Lefebvre goes on to say, "The powers that slumbered within them have been suppressed so that a 'few might be developed more fully and multiply through their union with those of others. The very turmoil of the streets has something repulsive'" (Lefebvre, 2016, p. 7, quoting Engels). The story of what redevelopment has done to economically and racially disfranchised queer people as well as the larger communities from which they come reveals another story – one about how city planners and elites have tried to suppress the powers that have dwelled within these communities, powers that at one point they could exercise in the city's neighborhoods and on its streets.

FOUR

The multidimensional character of violence

Walter Benjamin famously argued in "On the Concept of History," "The tradition of the oppressed teaches us that the 'state of emergency' in which we live is not the exception but the rule" (Benjamin, 2003, p. 392). Benjamin went on to argue that we need a conception of history that can hold the unexceptional nature of states of emergency within awareness. He continued by arguing that we need to bring about a "real state of emergency" that could challenge the everyday reality of fascism. That challenge could only commence once people ceased to take something that is a historical contrivance as a historical given. As he said, "One reason fascism has a chance is that, in the name of progress, its opponents treat it as a historical norm."

This book has been a critique of the idea of social progress, particularly as it tries to claim and distort queer history. To this end, the book has endeavored to illustrate how, as queer sexuality has been normalized, it has extended the regulations and exclusions of state and capital. As the mainstreaming of queerness

114

has extended those regulations and exclusions, it has also extended forms of social violence. In their article "Reclaiming Our Lineage: Organized Queer, Gender-Nonconforming, and Transgender Resistance to Police Violence," trans writers Che Gosset, Reina Gosset, and A. J. Lewis point to how this mainstreaming has also narrowed and obscured queer history's relationship to the issue of state and police violence:

> The riots that erupted at the Stonewall Bar on Christopher Street on the night of June 28, 1969, like the one at San Francisco's Compton Cafeteria in 1966, signaled a real turning point in queer activism. And yet, rather than being narrated as an urgent act of resistance and rebellion against state violence, the story of the Stonewall riot has been refashioned into a homonormative tale of the LGBT community's first proud public proclamation of gay identity and rejection of social stigma. The Compton Cafeteria riot was all but erased from mainstream LGBT history, obscuring the fact that the individuals who fought back against the police that evening were not simply members of San Francisco's gay community, but were also those who most often have to resist police oppression: street youth, gay and lesbian people of color, sex workers, drag queens, transgender, and gender-nonconforming people. (Gossett, Gossett, and Lewis, 2011–12)

The above passage points to how a one-dimensional explanation of queer struggles is not only about the containment of social change. One-dimensional explanations also work to obscure the workings of and the historical challenges to systemic forms of violence.

Taking inspiration from Benjamin, Gossett, Gossett, and Lewis, this chapter argues that given the unexceptional nature of violence, we must attain to a conception of history in which racial, gender, sexual, and class exploitations are analyzed as forces that constitute the quotidian nature of violence. To do so we have to turn our attention to the multidimensional and intersectional social struggles that have made up the center of this book. Doing so is important to rebut the common presumption that those struggles were simply expressions of a liberal multiculturalism interested primarily in advertising the wonders of differences of race, gender, and sexuality. These multidimensional and intersectional struggles in fact issued powerful critiques of state and capital as both envoys of social progress and justifiers of social violence. In doing so, those struggles pointed to the ways in which a single-issue politics of sexuality obscured rather than illuminated the forms of violence that were shaping queer and trans life. This chapter argues that understanding contemporary social violence requires intersectional frameworks that have always attempted to understand the workings of race, class, gender, and sexuality in relation to structural and personal forms of violence. In doing so, the chapter argues that a multidimensional politics has been a powerful analytical framework for understanding and challenging state violence. In contrast, one-dimensional analyses have obscured social and institutional forms of violence and continue to conceal the ways in which intersectional orientations were developed in order to illuminate and challenge those forms of violence. The chapter shows that in contrast, women of color feminism and queer of color critical formations have provided alternative models of how violence is not exceptional to but constitutive of the US nation-state and how single-issue models have historically relatively narrow conceptions of violence.

The pulse of violence

American Studies scholar Christina Hanhardt has argued that the normalization of gay politics has promoted analyses that prevent an awareness of racialized and class violence, for people of color but in particular for queers and trans of color people. As she argues, "Since [the 1970s], as mainstream LGBT activism has homed in on the project of inclusion, it has simultaneously maintained an analytic separation of sexual and gender normativity from racism and political economy via the use of metaphor and the advocacy of privatization and criminalization" (Hanhardt, 2013, p. 187). With this Hanhardt suggests the kinds of one-dimensional formulations that this book has been analyzing, formulations that, in their promotion of market forces, have also expanded the conditions of violence for vulnerable populations.

One incident that illustrates the analytic separation that Hanhardt invokes and the conditions of violence that such a separation fosters can be seen in the media coverage of the mass murder at Orlando's Pulse Nightclub, a gay bar and dance club. On Sunday June 12, 2016, a lone gunman named Omar Mateen entered the Pulse Nightclub and with a semi-automatic rifle and a pistol proceeded to shoot the nightclub's patrons. He killed forty-nine people and wounded fifty-eight. The most common interpretations of Mateen's murder spree explained his actions in terms of his declared allegiance to ISIS (so-called Islamic State) and the homophobia presumed by that allegiance. For instance, the *New York Times* reported, "'It was the worst act of terrorism on American soil since Sept. 11, 2001, and the deadliest attack on a gay target in the nation's history'" (Alvarez and Pérez-Peña, 2016). President Obama seemed to endorse this interpretation as well, stating, "'In the face of hatred and violence, we will love one another ... We will not give in to fear or turn against each other. Instead we will stand united as Americans to protect our people and defend our nation, and to take action against those who threaten us'" (Alvarez and Pérez-Peña, 2016). Donald Trump used the occasion to argue that Muslims should be barred from entering the country's borders. Hillary Clinton called for a "redoubling" of efforts to stop terrorism in the US and abroad (Alvarez and Pérez-Peña, 2016). All of the comments assumed not only the exceptional but also the foreign nature of homophobia within the US, doing so through what Jasbir Puar has identified as the "very specific production of terrorist bodies against properly queer subjects" (Puar, 2007, p. xiii). This set of assumptions attempted to shut down critiques of the constitutive role that homophobia has played in US society.

We might read the official responses to the murders as an example of how a single-issue and normative interpretation of sexuality has made its way into mainstream political and media contexts. The responses cast the incident as an attack on "all gays" regardless of racial and class background, and work to frame the US as a beacon of social progress where matters of queer sexuality are concerned, implicitly framing the Middle East as an unadulterated hotbed of homophobia. As such these interpretations illustrate the ways in which single-issue notions of sexuality promote the state as the benevolent guardian of minority life.

While mainstream news sources may have tried to frame what happened at the Pulse within an Islamophobic narrative that casts Mateen as a homophobic terrorist, other interpretations drew on frameworks that located Mateen squarely within the all too familiar discourses of patriarchal masculinity. For instance, queer theorist Jack Halberstam addressed the media's single-issue orientation to the murders, writing, "In a recent response to the shootings of Latino gay men and others in the Pulse Nightclub in Orlando Florida, June 12, the *Atlantic* ran an article claiming that violence against LGBT people in the U.S. was all too common and was even more common than violence directed at minorities" (Halberstam, 2016). As Halberstam notes, that argument was then taken up in a soon-to-follow article in the *New York Times*. Halberstam identifies the argument's author as Mark Potok, a senior fellow at the Southern Poverty Law Center, who stated in the *Atlantic* article, "'LGBT people are more than twice as likely to be the target of a violent hate-crime than Jews or black people'" (Halberstam, 2016). Halberstam then challenges Potok, arguing, "This is an interesting claim in that it presumes both that LGBT people are neither

Jews nor Blacks and that killers target people on the basis of only one strand of hatred! It also creates a specious hierarchy of violence in which white LGBT people are cast as more vulnerable than other minority groups" (Halberstam, 2016).

Challenging this one-dimensional interpretation of the violence visited upon the clubgoers, Halberstam states, "But these killings were highly specific and as new material surfaces on Omar Mateen's tortured relationship to his own sexuality, we want to challenge this sense of an amorphous homophobic threat that separates homophobic violence out from the particular, convulsive expressions of racialized hate" (Halberstam, 2016). The "new material" which undermined the narrative of Mateen as a terrorist for ISIS included testimony from men who said that Mateen had messaged them via apps like Grindr and Jack'd as well as from another man who claimed to be Mateen's lover. According to the latter, what was advertised – by Mateen and others – as an attack in the name of the so-called Islamic State was in fact the act of a man rejected by potential and actual lovers at the Pulse. Halberstam's correction is significant in that it demonstrates how a single-issue interpretation of LGBT violence as having only to do with sexuality cannot illuminate the particular and rampant forms of violence visited upon LGBT people of color.

By turning to the long history of toxic masculinities' relationships to homophobia, Halberstam disrupts the narrative that displaces homophobia onto Muslim communities and refutes the myth of American exceptionalism. Halberstam writes, "In other queer clubs, on other nights, other bodies have fallen victim to the toxic masculinities that imagine violence as the solution to shifts in the status quo that might shake up hierarchies of sex and gender. But on this night, in this club, the target of steroid fueled, militaristic, narcissistic, deeply conflicted masculinity was a group of mostly Latino gay men" (Halberstam, 2016). And in contrast to the narrative that tried to suture Mateen's actions to his identifications with ISIS, the novelist Justin Torres places the violence of that night within the everyday poisons of homophobia, racism, colonialism, and xenophobia in his article "In Praise of Latin Night at the Queer Club" (Torres, 2016). Rather than being monopolized by a single national or religious formation, homophobia, as Torres suggests, extends to them all. In a moment in which there was every effort to sustain an Islamophobic narrative, the most critical versions of queerness arose to bear witness to the breadth of homophobic aggression beyond national and religious boundaries. Indeed, instead of understanding Mateen's violence as a foreign encroachment, it would be more accurate to read it as a homegrown event enabled by the violence that underlies the racial, gender, sexual, and class violences of the US nation-state.

In his own article about the killings, Torres also challenged the separation of homophobic violence from racial hate. As he stated,

> Outside, there's a world that politicizes every aspect of your identity. There are preachers, of multiple faiths, mostly self-identified Christians, condemning you to hell. Outside, they call you an abomination. Outside, there is a news media that acts as if there are two sides to a debate over trans people using public bathrooms. Outside, there is a presidential candidate who has built a platform on erecting a wall between the United States and Mexico – and not only do people believe that crap is possible, they believe it is necessary. Outside, Puerto Rico is still a colony, being allowed to drown in debt, to suffer, without the right to file for bankruptcy, to protect itself. Outside, there are more than 100 bills targeting you, your choices, your people, pending in various states. (Torres, 2016)

Like Halberstam, Torres accounts for the murders at the nightclub not by explaining them in terms of Mateen's pathologies or external terrorist threats but by locating them within social forces that are at work within the

US. He invokes the homophobia actively produced in churches, the media-supported homophobia that normalizes transphobia as the entitlement of people opposed to transgender kids and adults, the anti-immigrant racism that characterized and energized the Trump campaign, and the ongoing colonization of Puerto Rico. With this, Torres not only rebuts an Islamophobic narrative that casts nations and people from the Middle East as the other of the freedom-loving US, but also provides a glimpse of the varieties of violence that constitute the contemporary US.

Torres suggests that an awareness of the quotidian and multidimensional nature of violence within the US constitutes Latinx queer identity. As he says, "You have known violence. You have known violence. You are queer and you are brown and you have known violence. You have known a masculinity, a machismo, stupid with its own fragility" (Torres, 2016). Instead of reading Mateen's toxic masculinity as something exceptional, Torres casts it as something familiar to Latinx queer men.

Halberstam's and Torres's comments refer to the inability of single-issue analyses to comprehend certain forms of violence, particularly when those forms are visited upon queer of color and trans of color communities and peoples. Moreover, these writers' remarks emphasize the everyday threat of violence against people of color, in general, and queers and trans of color, in particular. This quotidian nature of violence undermines the claim that the US is a nation progressive on questions of sexuality and race and that homophobia and transphobia are nuisances that dog less "developed" nations. In the next section, we will see how a multidimensional analysis emerged out of women of color and queer of color contexts, to address the inability of single-issue analyses to apprehend certain forms of violence and as a way to illuminate the everyday violence that certain political, economic, and activist constituencies could not and refused to see.

Intersectionality and the address to violence

The overlapping histories of women of color feminism and queer of color critical formations can be understood as a development that attempted to address occurrences like the one that took place at the Pulse Nightclub. We might understand women of color feminist analytics, in particular, as ones that tried to provide alternatives to single-issue analytics, precisely because those analytics could not apprehend and address the forms of violence with which women of color were contending. Indeed, it was the everyday but unacknowledged racist and heteropatriarchal violence within US society that occasioned activist, artistic, and scholarly responses to how that violence was jeopardizing cisgendered women of color's lives. This violence was unacknowledged not only among lay observers but among scholars and activists as well.

For instance, the Combahee River Collective's 1979 pamphlet "8 Black Women: Why Did They Die?" (later published as "Why Did They Die? A Document of Black Feminism" in the journal *Radical America*) provided an early illustration of not only the critique of ideologies of discreteness but what was at stake in that critique: the literal lives of women against heteropatriarchal violence and the larger society's refusal to end that violence and value the lives of women minoritized by race, gender, and poverty. The pamphlet was written in response to the murders of six black women in Boston beginning in January of 1979. By June of that year the numbers had risen to twelve black women and one white woman. The Collective used the pamphlet to address an ideology of discreteness that was informing mainstream black activist responses. As they stated in the pamphlet, "In the Black community the murders have often been talked about as solely racial or racist crimes. It's true that the victims were all Black and that Black people have always been targets of racist violence in this society, but they were also *all women*" (Combahee River Collective, 1979, p. 44). The pamphlet rebutted the notion that the attacks were "solely racial" and therefore drew attention to the single-issue ideology that was informing that response. To do so they questioned the presumption that this ideology could adequately address the multiple contours of violence against black women in the city. With this maneuver, they helped to both identify the workings of one-dimensional ideologies within a progressive formation, and to show how that ideology was inadequate to the task of assessing the social world's brutality. As they stated, "As Black women who are feminists we are struggling against all racist, sexist, heterosexist and class oppression. We know that we have no hopes of ending the particular crisis and violence against women in our community until we identify *all* of its causes, including sexual oppression" (Combahee River Collective, 1979, p. 46).

The stakes of their intervention were developed out of an awareness that black women were literally at risk of being murdered. As Barbara Smith wrote in 1979, in her own reflections on that moment, "That winter and spring were a time of great demoralization, anger, sadness and fear for many Black women in Boston, including myself. It was also for me a time of some of the most intensive and meaningful political organizing

I have ever done" (Smith, 1994, p. 315). Discussing the ways in which a multidimensional (i.e. intersectional) analysis was created within this context, Smith argues,

> The Black feminist political analysis and practice the Combahee River Collective had developed since 1974 enabled us to grasp both the sexual-political and racial-political implications of the murders and positioned us to be the link between the various communities that were outraged: Black people, especially Black women; other women of color; and white feminists, many of whom were also lesbians.

In her 1985 article "Racial Ethnic Women's Labor: The Intersection of Race, Gender, and Class Oppression," sociologist Evelyn Nakano Glenn, working with the Inter-University Group Researching the Intersection of Race and Gender, argued for the creation of an analytical framework that could address overlapping stratifications. She wrote, "A necessary next step [in researching racial ethnic women] is the development of theoretical and conceptual frameworks for analyzing the interaction of racial and gender stratification" (Nakano Glenn, 1985, p. 87). Recognizing the need for an analytical model that could address the multiple vulnerabilities of certain communities, Nakano Glenn wrote, "Although the 'double' (race, gender) and 'triple' (race, gender, class) oppression of racial ethnic women are widely acknowledged, no satisfactory theory has been developed to analyze what happens when these systems of oppression intersect" (1985, p. 87). As Nakano Glenn states, it was stratification and oppression that motivated a mode of analysis that would speak to the circumstances of women of color. By focusing on the question of stratification, Nakano Glenn suggested that creating an intersectional analytic was motivated by the problem of how best to assess the overlaps between stratified modes of violence, an intellectual quest that was necessary given that the dominant social scientific paradigm was to keep those stratifications separate even as they were intersecting in real people's lives.

In "Demarginalizing the Intersection of Race and Sex: A Black Feminist Critique of Antidiscrimination Doctrine, Feminist Theory and Antiracist Politics," the 1989 article by Kimberlé Crenshaw that is credited with having coined the category "intersectionality," Crenshaw demonstrates how a single-issue analytic was operating in the legal terrain. In the article, for instance, she discusses the case *DeGraffenreid v General Motors*, explaining it as follows:

> five Black women brought suit against General Motors, alleging that the employer's seniority system perpetuated

the effects of past discrimination against Black women. Evidence adduced at trial revealed that General Motors simply did not hire Black women prior to 1964 and that all of the Black women hired after 1970 lost their jobs in a seniority-based layoff during a subsequent recession. (Crenshaw, 1989, p. 141)

Granting summary judgment for the defendant, the court stated, "Thus, this lawsuit must be examined to see if it states a cause of action for race discrimination, sex discrimination or alternatively either, but not a combination of both." As such, the court used the law to legitimate a one-dimensional ideology in relation to the circumstances of black women as workers. In doing so, the courts raised white women and black men as the respective ideals of gender and race discrimination, effectively occluding black women's exploitation in the workplace and closing any door to legal redress. As Crenshaw stated, "The court's refusal in *DeGraffenreid* to acknowledge that Black women encounter combined race and sex discrimination implies that the boundaries of sex and race discrimination doctrine are defined respectively by white women's and black men's experiences" (Crenshaw, 1989, pp. 142–3).

In her article "Mapping the Margins: Intersectionality, Identity Politics and Violence Against Women of

Color," Crenshaw identifies the consequences of one-dimensional thinking for anti-racist and feminist activism, particularly in how this thinking aggravated the political lives of women of color. She writes, "The need to split one's political energies between two opposing groups is a dimension of intersectional disempowerment that men of color and white women seldom confront. Indeed, their specific raced and gendered experiences, although intersectional, often define as well as confine the interests of the entire group" (Crenshaw, 1993, p. 1252). As the experiences of men of color and white women became the ways to understand race and gender respectively, these people refused to see the other dimensions that were shaping race and gender. As Crenshaw notes, this directly impacted the nature of anti-racist and feminist political visions: "For example, racism as experienced by people of color who are of a particular gender – male – tends to determine the parameters of anti-racist strategies, just as sexism as experienced by women who are of a particular race – white – tends to ground the women's movement" (Crenshaw, 1993, p. 1252). Imposing a one-dimensional model of race and gender on anti-racist and feminist social movements, thus, narrows the diagnostic powers of those movements. As Crenshaw puts it, "The problem is not simply that both discourses fail women of color by not acknowledging the 'additional' issue of race or of patriarchy but that the discourses are often inadequate even to the discrete tasks of articulating the full dimension of racism and sexism." This produces a situation in which "anti-racism and feminism are limited, even on their own terms" (Crenshaw, 1993, p. 1252). Hence, the discrete contours of a racial logic operating within the feminist movement, a gendered logic constituting the anti-racist movement, and a monolithic discourse informing the legal sphere – all of which withheld the lives of women of color from both speculation and redress – prompted the emergence of intersectional work.

Subsequent work within queer studies has attempted to show how intersectional and multidimensional models were necessary to understand the devaluation of trans life as well. In his book *Normal Life: Administrative Violence, Critical Trans Politics, and the Limits of Law*, legal theorist Dean Spade identifies the multidimensional forms of inequality and violence that transgender people have to negotiate, writing, "Trans populations are disproportionately poor because of employment discrimination, family rejection, and difficulty accessing school, medical care, and social services" (Spade, 2011, p. 89). The consequences of poverty, transphobia, educational and medical insecurities, and administrative violence can be seen, according to Spade, in the specific ways that transgender people are affected by criminalization, police surveillance, and incarceration. He writes, "These factors increase our rate of participation in criminalized work to survive, which, combined with police profiling, produces high levels of criminalization. Trans people in prisons face severe harassment, medical neglect and violence in both men's and women's facilities" (Spade, 2011, p. 89).

As the gay rights agenda promotes hate crime legislation as a way to address violence against transgender folks, it applies a one-dimensional model that fails to see the ways in which expanding police powers will only make the lives of transgender folks more vulnerable. Within men's prisons, for instance, transgender people are often subjected to "forced prostitution, sexual slavery, sexual assault and other violence" (Spade, 2011, p. 89). In women's facilities, transgender people are likewise often subjected to "sexual assault and rape, most frequently at the hands of correctional staff" (p. 89). In women's facilities, Spade writes, prisoners "perceived as too masculine by prison staff are often at significantly higher risk of harassment and enhanced punishment, including psychologically damaging isolation, for alleged violations against rules of homosexual contact" (Spade, 2011, pp. 89–90). As Spade says, "Since the criminal punishment system is a significant source of racialized-gendered violence, increasing its resources and punishment capacity will not reduce violence against trans people" (Spade, 2011, p. 90). Discussing the ways that anti-violence initiatives for transgender persons becomes the justification for increasing the capacities of the carceral state, Spade goes on to say, "A new mandate to punish transphobic people is added to the arsenal of justifications for a system that primarily locks up and destroys the lives of poor people, people of color, indigenous people, people with disabilities, and immigrants, and that uses gender-based violence as one of its daily tools of discipline against people of all genders" (Spade, 2011, p. 90).

In *Social Death: Racialized Rightlessness and the Criminalization of the Unprotected*, ethnic studies scholar Lisa Cacho defines violence as a way of ordering humanity and not only as a series of acts visited upon people. She writes, "human value is made intelligible through racialized, sexualized, spatialized, and state-sanctioned violences" (Cacho, 2012, p. 4). In the context of the incarceration, criminalization, and murders of marginalized queers and trans people, their personhood is made intelligible as a source of devaluation and as the object of legitimate violence. Cacho's framework underlines one of the implicit arguments that runs throughout all these chapters: the denigration of racially and economically marginalized queer and trans populations has been necessary in producing the most exclusionary forms of queer politics and the most aggressive neoliberal policies within the US.

I have provided this rather lengthy literature review to illustrate how even within the great range of women of color and queer of color critical work, a consistent through line has been a concern with the violences that have gone unacknowledged by entities committed to single-issue politics. As such we can look to this work for analyses that can help us assess the forms of violence that make up present-day contests with neoliberal, racial, and colonial states. To state this differently, women of color feminist and queer of color works have been naming the forms of violence that we identify now as "neoliberal" for quite some time.

If neoliberalism denotes the upward redistribution of resources away from the people who need those resources to those who require them for the augmentation of their wealth, then neoliberalism would need to obscure the violence done to disfranchised communities and people. It is within this context that the insights and analytical models developed by women of color and queer of color feminists can help illuminate the modes of violence produced and obscured by neoliberalism. In their own ways Halberstam's and Torres's articles point to the ways in which the exigencies of race, class, and immigration shaped the lives of the clubgoers at the Pulse Nightclub – that their existences were not merely shaped by a one-dimensional notion of sexuality. They were impacted by an array of neoliberal and colonial exigencies that included and exceeded sexuality. As those urgencies denote a variety of social, economic, cultural, and political contexts, they require multidimensional analyses for their apprehension. As we will see in the next section, a fully achieved multidimensional and intersectional understanding of violence must also be a way of understanding US and Western state formations and their relationships to violence.

Fascism and the violence of the nation-state

Tellingly, Torres invokes the history of state violence when he argues that "Outside, Puerto Rico is still a colony, being allowed to drown in debt, to suffer, without the right to file for bankruptcy, to protect itself" (Torres, 2016). Torres's invocation reminds us that violence must never be understood as only part of the internal workings of the nation but as part of its external relationships as well. As the media responses attempted to externalize the murders at the nightclub onto an external threat, casting predominantly Muslim nations in the Middle

East as the primary aggressors on the world stage, Torres's reminder of Puerto Rico's status disturbs that assumption. Instead, it raises the US's history of violence that has proceeded under the rubric of "foreign policy." As Torres writes, "The media will spin the conversation away from homegrown homophobic terrorism to a general United States vs. Islamist narrative. Mendacious, audacious politicians – Republicans who vote against queer rights, against gun control – will seize on this massacre, twist it for support of their agendas" (Torres, 2016).

Torres's remarks invoke the US government's use of homophobia as justification for expanding the military–industrial complex. In his book *Freedom with Violence*, Chandan Reddy draws attention to the Matthew Shepard and James Byrd, Jr., Hate Crimes Prevention Act of 2009, "which added sexual orientation and gender identity to the list of federally defined hate crimes" (Reddy, 2011, p. 3). Named after two victims of hate crimes, the act "extended the definition of federal hate crimes from crimes motivated by a victim's actual or perceived race, religion, ethnicity or nationality to include crimes targeting a victim's actual or perceived sexual orientation, gender identity, or disability" (Reddy, 2011, p. 3). The act was adopted as an amendment to the National Defense Authorization Act (NDAA), which in 2010 appropriated "$680 billion dollars to the Department of

Defense – during the worst recession and job market in the United States since the end of the Great Depression and the second world war" (Reddy, 2011, p. 2). Passed during US wars in the Middle East and South Asia, the NDAA "appropriated funding for the continued use of unmanned US drone strikes and bombings in countries that the United States is not officially at war with, such as Pakistan, disrespecting their national sovereignty and inflicting civilian deaths" (Reddy, 2011, p. 4). Reddy goes on to argue that the passage of the NDAA was regarded as an unmitigated success by "the Democratic Party, liberal and progressive groups and constituencies, and national gay and lesbian rights organizations" (Reddy, 2011, p. 4) because of its recognition of lesbian, gay, bisexual, transgender, queer (LGBTQ) rights and protections.

Writing in 2017, Spade argued, "The last few years have witnessed unprecedented visibility of trans people in popular culture alongside a strong backlash against trans people. The right is targeting trans people with bills to criminalize trans people's use of bathrooms and public education campaigns that promote fear and hatred" (Spade, 2017). At the same time, Spade warns, trans visibility is also being used for US military expansion. He writes, "But these aren't the only steps the right wing is taking in regard to trans people. The right is also leveraging trans issues as a tool for promoting right-wing security and military agendas" (Spade, 2017).

The sociologist Max Weber argued, in his 1918 address entitled "Politics as a Vocation," that "[Force] is a means specific to the state ... Today the relation between the state and violence is an especially intimate one ... Today ..., we have to say that a state is the only human community that (successfully) claims *the monopoly of the legitimate use of physical force within a given territory*" (Weber, 1946, p. 78). In the twenty-first century we are witnessing the use of homosexuality and transgender identity as resources to promote the state's capacities to legitimate state violence abroad. This can only be done within an ideological horizon in which homosexuality and transgender identities have been severed from critiques of the state and imperialism. More pointedly, the creation and ascendancy of a one-dimensional ideology about queer sexuality has helped to usher in this moment in which queerness and trans identity are compatible with state violence.

As Reddy and Spade suggest, the dangerous context in which queer and trans visibility receives state recognition is one constituted by the expansion of the military–industrial complex and the dissemination of global warfare, particularly in the Middle East. Discussing the relationship between global warfare and the establishment of national identity, the historian Eric Hobsbawm wrote that one of the criteria that "allowed a people to be firmly classed as a nation" (Hobsbawm, 1990, p. 37) is "a proven capacity for conquest. There is nothing like being an imperial people to make a population conscious of its collective existence as such" (Hobsbawm, 1990, p. 38). Inasmuch as queer and trans folks seek to bring their identities into alignment with the military–industrial complex, they beg not just for general recognition as human beings but as acknowledged members of an imperial body. It is that body that Torres invokes in the US colonization of Puerto Rico. Acquired during the Spanish American War by the US, Puerto Rico allows the US to become part of the international colonial momentum that, as Hobsbawm argued, "provided the Darwinian proof of evolutionary success as a species" (Hobsbawm, 1990, p. 38). We can think of Spade's argument about trans incorporation into the military as a comment about the effort to make transgender people part of the ongoing twenty-first-century "evolutionary success [of the imperial] species." As homophobic and transphobic violence becomes a justification for the imperial expansion of the military–industrial complex, it reveals its role in the expansion of neoliberal agendas. If, again, neoliberalism represents the redistribution of resources to the elite, then the expansion of military powers in the name of the most vulnerable is neoliberalism par excellence.

Since the beginning of the Trump presidency, we are now in a moment in which that expansion takes place through a "steroid fueled, militaristic, narcissistic, deeply conflicted masculinity" (Halberstam, 2016) that does not solely belong to Omar Mateen. It is quickly becoming the general disposition of the US nation-state and cannot be simply projected onto nations outside the US either. By way of example, the increase in the number of white nationalist groups in the US, the burning of mosques, and the desecration of Jewish cemeteries, among other incidents, suggest that what happened at the Pulse was not an isolated event but part of a wave of aggression that implicates not only ISIS but the US as well. In his study of international socialist movements and their response to the global growth of fascism, the British historian G. D. H. Cole argued,

> Before Hitler, Mussolini had built Italian Fascism round the cult of the nation, conceived as essentially an assertive power group, activated by a collective "social egoism" in its dealings with the rest of the world, and inspired by a cult of "violence" that exalted violence and cruelty into virtues when they were manifested in the cause of the nation so conceived of. (Cole, 1960, p. 6)

We see the versatility and destructiveness of this social egoism as it attempts to make virtues out of transphobia, homophobia, anti-Semitism, xenophobia, Islamophobia, settler colonialism, anti-black racism, and ableism. Rather than relegating a social problem to one region of the world, the killings call attention to how varieties of nationalism around the globe are providing the ground on which fascism might have a brand new and multi-routed run. The most developed barometers for understanding how masculinity, imperial expansion, and domestic violence are imbricated in our everyday existence have come from intersectional frameworks. Those frameworks are urgently needed as those imbrications open onto authoritarian horizons.

Conclusion: The historical assumptions of multidimensional queer politics

This book has attempted to provide a history and a theory of what happened to gay liberation. It began as a reconsideration of what took place that night at the Stonewall Inn, taking a trans woman of color at her word when she said that the rebellion of that evening was not the spontaneous eruption of depoliticized actors but was in fact an event informed by a series of movements that shaped militant queens. This book's theorization of gay liberation as having multidimensional rather than single-issue and one-dimensional beginnings proceeds from that retelling.

The book then moved to consider how political and economic forces among queers themselves arose to discipline that multidimensional origin and replace it with a narrative that would naturalize a one-dimensional interpretation of sexuality, an interpretation that would work to sever sexuality from critiques of race, gender, capitalism, and colonialism and thereby make sexuality the handmaiden of state and capital. After showing how a one-dimensional interpretation of sexuality was a driving force behind a specific political and economic agenda, the book turned to the ways in which that agenda has enabled the neoliberal transformation of urban space, a transformation that has caused cities around the US and the world to betray the very people that have made cities such as New York and San Francisco legendary in the first place. Then, in an assessment of what politics, capital, and urban locales have done to the most vulnerable in the name of the mainstreaming of queer culture, the book turned to the ultimate violence of one-dimensional interpretations of queer liberation. In this conclusion the book now comes to the logical question of what then is the status of radical queer politics in the shadow of this history. The multidimensional forms of analysis and activism that this book has engaged provide the seeds of an answer.

In the conclusion to *One-Dimensional Man*, Marcuse provided a gloss on the seemingly indomitable encroachments of advanced industrial society, writing

The enchained possibilities of advanced industrial society are: development of the productive forces on an enlarged scale, extension of the conquest of nature, growing satisfaction of needs for a growing number of people, creation of new needs and faculties. But these possibilities are gradually being realized through means and institutions which cancel their liberating potential, and this process affects not only the means but also the ends. (Marcuse, 1991, p. 255)

Given this book's discussion of what social progress around queer sexuality has meant, it is hard not to consider similarly how our society has also "enchained" the possibilities for queerness. Indeed, queerness has found its way into the political and economic mainstream, producing opportunities that were unprecedented decades before. But like the possibilities that Marcuse wrote about, those opportunities have been realized through means and institutions that have actively worked to cancel the broad and liberating potential of intersectional and multidimensional struggles.

Marcuse sounds a note of hope in those who, because they have not been lifted up in the tide of progress, participate in what he calls the Great Refusal. He writes, "However, underneath the conservative popular base is the substratum of the outcasts and outsiders, the exploited and persecuted of other races and other colors, the unemployed and the unemployable. They exist outside the democratic process; their life is the most immediate and the most real need for ending intolerable conditions and institutions" (Marcuse, 1991, p. 256). About them he goes on to say, "Thus their opposition is revolutionary even if their consciousness is not ... But the chance is that, in this period, the historical extremes may meet again: the most advanced consciousness of humanity, and its most exploited force. It is nothing but a chance" (1991, pp. 256–7).

Here Marcuse perhaps points to a principle that the multidimensional movements evoked in this book have gestured toward: the need to seize upon a chance as the opening toward a possible future. In fact, this book has implicitly looked at those movements as the repositories of certain historical assumptions about multidimensional queer politics. A primary assumption is that any given moment can go in the direction of several different futures, that the present is not preordained to any given end. Isn't this one of the points of Stonewall: the intentional selection of a possible future and the ability to maneuver immediate circumstances so as to try to yield that future? The multidimensional understanding of Stonewall says that our hope and our politics lie in our capacity to seize the chance opportunity for a broad array of interventions.

Marcuse ends his conclusion and his book with a quote from his former colleague Walter Benjamin. The quote reads "It is only for the sake of those without hope that hope is given to us." In Benjamin's classic essay "On the Concept of History," he gestured toward memories and images as the figures of chance that could open up new political and social possibilities. He said,

> Articulating the past historically does not mean recognizing it the way "it really was." It means appropriating a memory as it flashes up in a moment of danger. Historical materialism wishes to hold fast that image of the past which unexpectedly appears to the historical subject in a moment of danger. The danger threatens both the content of the tradition and those who inherit it. For both, it is one and the same thing: the danger of becoming the tool of the ruling classes. (Benjamin, 2003, p. 391)

For Benjamin, historical materialists must do their best to grab hold of memory, an entity that is by its nature momentary. The historical materialist must do this because the memory – even in a flash – has the potential to disrupt power's hold. This book has attempted to grab hold of those fleeting instances in which multidimensional queer formations were trying to prevent queerness from becoming the tool of ruling classes. In doing so those formations presented liberatory politics as a confrontation with and a manipulation of chance.

Another historical assumption implied in this book is that queer history can be the basis of political theorizing. Moreover, this brand of political theorizing does not have to traffic in political theory's usual divisions of major and minor events. Discussing this, Benjamin said,

> The Chronicler who narrates events without distinguishing between major and minor ones acts in accord with the following truth: nothing that has ever happened should be regarded as lost to history. Of course only a redeemed mankind is granted the fullness of the past – which is to say, only for a redeemed mankind has its past become citable in all its moments. (Benjamin, 2003, p. 390)

In their discussion of this passage, Benjamin's biographers Howard Eiland and Mark Jennings argue, "Citability is the condition necessary for a living tradition" (Eiland and Jennings, 2014, p. 660). As such, this book has attempted to make multidimensional queer struggles citable so that our age – in Benjamin's words – may "strive anew to wrest tradition away from the conformism that is working to overpower it" (2003, p. 391). Also as such, the way that Sylvia Rivera remembers the Stonewall rebellion – as multidimensional and intersectional – should never be lost to history and must become a condition of our living tradition.

In the context of queer politics, the conformism that Benjamin warned against has taken the guise of a one-dimensional notion of liberation, one that works to separate struggles from one another in an effort to protect state and capital from critique and opposition. As an alternative to those maneuvers, multidimensional queer movements have illustrated a third historical assumption: the confluence of histories and political struggles. This historical assumption has pushed intersectional and multidimensional analyses and struggles among queers to strive for high levels of comprehensiveness. Analyses and activism emanating from those contexts have hence attempted to illuminate and maneuver various confluences that make up a social struggle. Consider, for instance, African American queer activist and writer Kenyon Farrow's critique of the discourse of gay rights in the global south:

> As long as Western liberal democracies can name "gay rights" as the new litmus test for an appropriate twenty-first century democracy, we can obsess about "anti-gay" legislation in Nigeria and say nothing about the violence and economic exploitation of the Shell Oil Company on the land and bodies of Nigerians. We can be seduced

by the international gay travel industry to visit "gay friendly" (and "post-racial paradise") Rio de Janeiro, and say nothing of the massive police violence and genocidal removal of blacks from favelas in preparation for the 2014 World Cup and 2016 Summer Olympics. (Farrow, 2011–12)

In this passage, Farrow points to how gay rights operate in a one-dimensional fashion that severs issues of homophobia from neocolonial exploitation and police violence. In a multidimensional approach, Farrow instead prioritizes the interrelatedness of social urgencies. In doing so, his remarks point to the need for a queer politics that can determine the collaborations between seemingly disparate issues.

Maneuvering those conjunctures is a simultaneously political and intellectual endeavor. As Marcuse observes, "The way in which a society organizes the life of its members involves an initial *choice* between historical alternatives which are determined by the inherited level of the material and intellectual culture" (Marcuse, 1991, p. xlviii). Put plainly, the clarity with which we understand an intellectual and political inheritance greatly determines whether we can identify and compel an alternative future. This last historical assumption assumes that intellectual culture is significant in the unfolding of history, that intellectual culture is partly what informs what people will do when they get to any crossroad that compels a decision between the alternative and the conventional. Knowing this clarifies the major difference between multidimensional struggles and their one-dimensional counterparts. While the latter are about the curtailment of historical agency and historical possibility, the former represent the effort to retain our agency as historical beings and to enlarge the conditions for real liberation, doing so through the constant accumulation of alternative struggles that we can cite and build upon.

1 I use the term "Latinx" as a non-binary alternative to "Latino" and "Latina" and to acknowledge the reality of gender non-conforming people in Latinx communities.

2 Indeed, scholars have turned their attention to the ways in which a dominant and Eurocentric narrative of Stonewall has fostered a misreading of queer formations in other countries (see for instance Manalansan, 1995, and Bacchetta, 2002).

Alvarez, L., and Pérez-Peña, R. (2016, June 12). Orlando Gunman Attacks Gay Nightclub. *New York Times*.

Bacchetta, P. (2002). Rescaling Transnational "Queerdom": Lesbian and "Lesbian" Identitary-Positionalities in Delhi in the 1980s. *Antipode* 34 (5), pp. 947–73.

Bacchetta, P. (2009). DYKETACTICS! Notes Towards an Un-Silencing. In T. A. Mecca (Ed.), *Smash the Church, Smash the State! The Early Years of Gay Liberation* (pp. 218–31). San Francisco, CA: City Lights Books.

Bedoz, E., Lewis, B., and Warshawsky, A. (1970). Dialogue. *Come Out! A Liberation Forum for the Gay Community* 1 (3), p. 13.

Benjamin, W. (2003). On the Concept of History. In H. Eiland and M. W. Jennings (Eds.), *Walter Benjamin: Selected Writings. Vol. 4: 1938–1940* (pp. 389–400). Cambridge, MA: Belknap Press.

Biron, L. (1976, Spring). The *Advocate*: Capitalist Manifesto. *The Gay Sunshine*. http://photos-biron.com/advocate.htm

Black Panther Party. (1995). Call for Revolutionary People's Constitutional Convention, September 7, 1970, Philadelphia, Pa. In P. S. Foner (Ed.), *The Black Panthers Speak* (pp. 267–71). New York, NY: Da Capo Press.

Cacho, L. M. (2012). *Social Death: Racialized Rightlessness and the Criminalization of the Unprotected*. New York: New York University Press.

Chasin, A. (2001). *Selling Out: The Gay and Lesbian Movement Goes to Market*. New York, NY: Palgrave Macmillan.

Bibliography

Chisholm, D. (2004). *Queer Constellations: Subcultural Space in the Wake of the City.* Minneapolis: University of Minnesota Press.

Cole, G. (1960). *A History of Socialist Thought, Volume V: Socialism and Fascism, 1931–1939.* London: Macmillan.

Combahee River Collective. (1979). Why Did They Die? A Document of Black Feminism. *Radical America* 13 (6), pp. 44–9.

Come Out! (1970a). Editorial. *Come Out! A Liberation Forum for the Gay Community* 1 (1), p. 1.

Come Out! (1970b). No Revolution Without Us. *Come Out! A Liberation Forum for the Gay Community* 1 (5), p. 17.

Come Out! (1970c). Questions that Have Never Been Answered to My Satisfaction. *Come Out! A Liberation Forum for the Gay Community* 2 (7b), p. 5.

Crenshaw, K. (1989). Demarginalizing the Intersection of Race and Sex: A Black Feminist Critique of Antidiscrimination Doctrine, Feminist Theory and Antiracist Politics. *University of Chicago Legal Forum* 1, pp. 139–67.

Crenshaw, K. (1993). Mapping the Margins: Intersectionality, Identity Politics, and Violence Against Women of Color. *Stanford Law Review* 43, pp. 1244–99.

Davison, S., Featherstone, D., and Schwarz, B. (2017). Introduction. In S. Davison, D. Featherstone, M. Rustin, and B. Schwarz (Eds.), *Selected Political Writings: The Great Moving Right Show and Other Essays* (pp. 1–15). Durham, NC: Duke University Press.

Delany, S. R. (1999). *Times Square Red, Times Square Blue.* New York: New York University Press.

D'Emilio, J. (2000). Cycles of Change, Questions of Strategy: The Gay and Lesbian Movement after Fifty Years. In C. Rimmerman, K. D. Wald, and C. Wilcox (Eds.), *The Politics of Gay Rights* (pp. 31–53). Chicago, IL: University of Chicago Press.

Dreger, C. (2002). Be Creative or Die. Salon.com. https://www.salon.com/2002/06/06/florida_22

Bibliography

Duggan, L. (2012). Beyond Marriage: Democracy, Equality, Kinship for a New Century. *S&F Online* 10 (1–2). http://sfonline.barnard. edu/a-new-queer-agenda/beyond-marriage-democracy-equality-and-kinship-for-a-new-century

Eiland, H. A., and Jennings, M. W. (2014). *Walter Benjamin: A Critical Life*. Cambridge, MA: Belknap Press.

Farrow, K. (2011–12). Afterword: A Future Beyond Equality. *Scholar and Feminist Online* 10.1–10.2. http://sfonline.barnard. edu/a-new-queer-agenda/afterword-a-future-beyond-equality

Florida, R. (2012). *The Rise of the Creative Class* (10th anniversary edn.). New York, NY: Basic Books.

Gavin, S. (1970). Is Socialism the Answer? *Come Out! A Liberation Forum for the Gay Community* 2 (7b), p. 5.

Gay Activists Alliance. (1972, March 2). *Constitution and Bylaws of the Gay Activists Alliance.* http://paganpressbooks.com/jpl/GAACONST.PDF

Gay Committee of Returned Brigadistas. (1971). Gay Brigadistas Letter to Come Out. *Come Out! A Liberation Forum for the Gay Community* 2 (7b), p. 5.

Goldsby, J. (1993). Queens of Language: *Paris Is Burning*. In M. Gever, J. Greyson, and P. Parmar (Eds.), *Queer Looks: Perspectives on Lesbian and Gay Film and Video* (pp. 108–15). London: Routledge.

Gossett, C., Gossett, R., and Lewis, A. J. (2011–12). Reclaiming Our Lineage: Organized Queer, Gender-Nonconforming, and Transgender Resistance to Police Violence. *Scholar and Feminist Online* 10.1–10.2. http://sfonline.barnard.edu/a-new-queer-agenda/ reclaiming-our-lineage-organized-queer-gender-nonconforming-and-transgender-resistance-to-police-violence

Halberstam, J. (2016, June 22). Who Are "We" After Orlando? *Bully Bloggers.* http://bullybloggers.wordpress.com/2016/06/22/who-are-we-after-orlando-by-jack-halberstam

Hall, S. (2017). Political Commitment. In S. Davison, D. Featherstone, M. Rustin, and B. Schwarz (Eds.), *Selected Political Writings: The*

Great Moving Right Show and Other Essays (pp. 85–106). Durham, NC: Duke University Press.

Hanhardt, C. B. (2013). *Safe Space: Gay Neighborhood History and the Politics of Violence.* Durham, NC: Duke University Press.

Haritaworn, J. (2015). *Queer Lovers and Hateful Others: Regenerating Violent Times and Places.* London: Pluto Press.

Harvey, D. (2007). Neoliberalism and the City. *Studies in Social Justice* 1 (1), pp. 1–13.

Highleyman, L. (2009). Kiyoshi Kuromiya: Integrating the Issues. In T. A. Mecca (Ed.), *Smash the Church, Smash the State! The Early Years of Gay Liberation* (pp. 17–21). San Francisco, CA: City Lights.

Hobsbawm, E. (1990). *Nations and Nationalism since 1780: Programme, Myth, Reality.* Cambridge: Cambridge University Press.

Hong, G. (2015). *Death Beyond Disavowal: The Impossible Politics of Difference.* Minneapolis: University of Minnesota Press.

Kissack, T. (1995). Freaking Fag Revolutionaries: New York's Gay Liberation Front, 1969–1971. *Radical History Review* 62, pp. 104–34.

Lefebvre, H. (2016). *Marxist Thought and the City* (R. Bononno, Trans.). Minneapolis: University of Minnesota Press.

Lekus, I. (2004). Queer Harvests: Homosexuality, the U.S. New Left, and the Venceremos Brigades to Cuba. *Radical History Review* 89, pp. 57–91.

Lorde, A. (2007). *Sister Outsider: Essays and Speeches by Audre Lorde.* Berkeley, CA: Crossing Press.

Manalansan, M. (1995). In the Shadows of Stonewall: Examining Gay Transnational Politics and the Diasporic Dilemma. In L. Lowe and D. Lloyd (Eds.), *The Politics of Culture in the Shadow of Capital* (pp. 485–505). Durham, NC: Duke University Press.

Manalansan, M. (2003). *Global Divas: Filipino Gay Men in the Diaspora.* Durham, NC: Duke University Press.

Marcuse, H. (1991). *One-Dimensional Man.* Boston, MA: Beacon.

Bibliography

Martello, L. L. (n.d.). Gay Power in Pay Power. *Gay Power Newspaper* 8. http://paganpressbooks.com/jpl/LEO.HTM

Martin, B. (1970). Letters to Marchers on Washington. *Come Out! A Liberation Forum for the Gay Community* 1 (2), p. 4.

Marx, K., and Engels, F. (1998). *The Communist Manifesto: A Modern Edition.* London: Verso.

Mecca, T. A. (2009). Introduction. In T. A. Mecca (Ed.), *Smash the Church, Smash the State! The Early Years of Gay Liberation* (pp. ix–xvi). San Francisco, CA: City Lights.

Melamed, J. (2011). *Represent and Destroy: Rationalizing Violence in the New Racial Capitalism.* Minneapolis: University of Minnesota Press.

Murphy, J. (1971). *Homosexual Liberation: A Personal View.* New York, NY: Praeger.

Nakano Glenn, E. (1985). Racial Ethnic Women's Labor: The Intersection of Race, Gender, and Class Oppression. *Review of Radical Political Economies* 17 (3), pp. 86–108.

Newton, H. (1970). A Letter from Huey P. Newton. *Come Out! A Liberation Forum for the Gay Community* 1 (5), p. 12.

Park, R. E., Burgess, E., and McKenzie, R. D. (1967). *The City.* Chicago, IL: University of Chicago Press.

Peck, J. (2005). Struggling with the Creative Class. *International Journal of Urban and Regional Research* 29 (4), pp. 740–70.

Potter, C. B. (2012). Paths to Political Citizenship: Gay Rights, Feminism, and the Carter Presidency. *Journal of Policy History* 24 (1), pp. 95–114.

Puar, J. (2007). *Terrorist Assemblages: Homonationalism in Queer Times.* Durham, NC: Duke University Press.

Rancière, J. (2004). *The Politics of Aesthetics* (G. Rockhill, Trans.). New York, NY: Continuum.

Reddy, C. (1997). Home, Houses, Nonidentity: *Paris Is Burning.* In R. M. George (Ed.), *Burning Down the House: Recycling Domesticity* (pp. 355–80). Boulder, CO: Westview Press.

Bibliography

Reddy, C. (2011). *Freedom with Violence: Race, Sexuality, and the U.S. State*. Durham, NC: Duke University Press.

Rivera, S. (2013a, March 12). "I'm Glad I was in the Stonewall Riot:" An Interview with Sylvia Rivera. *Street Transvestite Action Revolutionaries: Survival, Revolt, and Queer Antagonist Struggle*. https://untorellipress.noblogs.org/files/2011/12/STAR.pdf

Rivera, S. (2013b, March 12). Queens in Exile: The Forgotten Ones. *Street Transvestite Action Revolutionaries: Survival, Revolt, and Queer Antagonist Struggle*. https://untorellipress.noblogs.org/files/2011/12/STAR.pdf

Rivera, S. (2013c, March 12). Bitch on Wheels: A Speech by Sylvia Rivera, 2001. *Street Transvestite Action Revolutionaries: Survival, Revolt, and Queer Antagonist Struggle*. https://untorellipress.noblogs.org/files/2011/12/STAR.pdf

Rivera, S. (2013d, March 12). Y'all Better Quiet Down: Sylvia Rivera's Speech at Liberation Day, 1973. *Street Transvestite Action Revolutionaries: Survival, Revolt, and Queer Antagonist Struggle*. https://untorellipress.noblogs.org/files/2011/12/STAR.pdf

Robinson, C. J. (2000). *Black Marxism: The Making of the Black Radical Tradition*. Chapel Hill, NC, and London: University of North Carolina Press.

Roque Ramírez, H. (2003). "That's My Place!" Negotiating Racial, Sexual, and Gender Politics in San Francisco's Gay Latino Alliance, 1975–1983. *Journal of the History of Sexuality* 12 (2), pp. 224–58.

Said, E. (1994). *Representations of the Intellectual: The 1993 Reith Lectures*. New York, NY: Vintage.

Schreiner, M. (2011, December 14). An Army of Lovers Cannot Lose: The Occupation of NYU's Weinstein Hall. *Researching Greenwich Village History*. http://greenwichvillagehistory.wordpress.com/2011/12/14/an-army-of-lovers-cannot-lose-the-occupation-of-nyus-weinstein-hall

Sender, K. (2004). *Business Not Politics: The Making of the Gay Market*. New York, NY: Columbia University Press.

Shea, C. (2004, February 29). The Road to Riches? *Boston Globe*, D1.

Smith, B. (1994). The Boston Murders. In P. Bell-Scott (Ed.), *Life Notes: Personal Writings by Contemporary Black Women* (pp. 315–20). New York, NY: W. W. Norton.

Smith, N. M. (2015, September 25). Gay Rights Activists Give Their Verdict on Stonewall: "This Film is No Credit to the History it Purports to Portray." *The Guardian*. https://www.theguardian.com/film/2015/sep/25/stonewall-film-gay-rights-activists-give-their-verdict

Spade, D. (2011). *Normal Life: Administrative Violence, Critical Trans Politics and the Limits of Law*. Brooklyn, NY: South End Press.

Spade, D. (2017, April 5). The Right Wing is Leveraging Trans Issues to Promote Militarism. *Truth Out*. www.truth-out.org/opinion/item/40109-the-right-wing-is-leveraging-trans-issues-to-promote-militarism

STAR (2013, March 12). Street Transvestites for Gay Power: Statement on the 1971 NYU Occupation. *Street Transvestite Action Revolutionaries: Survival, Revolt, and Queer Antagonist Struggle*. https://untorellipress.noblogs.org/files/2011/12/STAR.pdf

Teal, D. (Ed.). (1971). *The Gay Militants*. New York, NY: Stein and Day.

Third World Gay Revolution. (1970a). Third World Gay Revolution: Who We Are/Quienes Somos. *Come Out! A Liberation Forum for the Gay Community* 1 (5), p. 12.

Third World Gay Revolution. (1970b). Third World Gay Revolution: The Oppressed Shall Not Become the Oppressor. *Come Out! A Liberation Forum for the Gay Community* 1 (5), p. 13.

Third World Gay Revolution. (1970c). Third World Gay Revolution: 16 Point Platform and Program. *Come Out! A Liberation Forum for the Gay Community* 1 (7), pp. 16–17.

Torres, J. (2016, June 13). In Praise of Latin Night at the Queer Club. *The Washington Post*. www.washingtonpost.com/opinions/in-praise-of-latin-night-at-the-queer-club/2016/06/13

Bibliography

University of Toronto Homophile Association. (1970). Letter to the Editors. *Come Out! A Liberation Forum for the Gay Community* 1 (3), p. 13.

Weber, M. (1946). Politics as a Vocation. In H. H. Girth and C. Wright Mills (Eds.), *Max Weber: Essays in Sociology* (pp. 77–128). New York, NY: Oxford University Press.

Woo, M. (2009). Stonewall was a Riot – Now We Need a Revolution. In T. A. Mecca (Ed.), *Smash the Church, Smash the State! The Early Years of Gay Liberation* (pp. 282–94). San Francisco, CA: City Lights.

Index

Index

Index

Index